Letters to Graduates

Brent D. Earles

BAKER BOOK HOUSE
Grand Rapids, Michigan 49516

For two priceless people
who will always hold a tender spot
in my heart,

Eugene and **Estelle Thomas.**

Thank you, Grandpa and Grandma,
for teaching me, loving me,
and for giving me
many of my childhood's
most wonderful memories.

Contents

Three from Dear John
(1, 2, and 3 John)

Postcards of Love
(Philemon, Jude)

Introduction

Do you mind if I act like we've already met? Can we dispense with the "How do you do's"? Would it be all right if we skip the formal stuff and get on with the show? I'd like to write you a series of letters as if we were old pen pals. Hope you have no problem with that.

The whole idea of "open letter" correspondence isn't a new one. Most of the New Testament Scriptures are composed of letters from an apostle to a church, or from one person to another. The nifty thing about this is that God has woven together all of those letters to form one big letter—a love letter—to us. Talk about mass circulation!

Anyway, the New Testament letters are going to be my point of reference as I prepare a mailbox full of messages for you. Hopefully this will inspire you to read the Epistles in God's Word, which are infinitely more important than my little memorandums.

Letters are a lot more personal than an ordinary book. Occasionally they are a bit *too* personal, but they are also more caring. Usually more thoughtful. Sometimes more direct. When matters are clearly stated, letters foster good relationships. But they are often cold and businesslike when the writer is not an open person. They can be precious and meaningful if the words are spoken with candor, sincerity, and warmth.

Our words reveal who we are and what we're like. On paper we have them for a lifetime, while a spoken word may be forgotten in a day, a month, or a year. (Perhaps this is why we might say, "The pen is mightier than the tongue.") It's not uncommon for special letters to become keepsakes. My wife, for instance, still has things I wrote to her fifteen years ago. My mother has kept messages I wrote as a child.

Part of the reason the Bible is so valuable is that it indelibly brings God's words to man. Printed on onionskin paper, but from God directly to mankind! Let that sink in. A note from your boyfriend is nice, a card from a friend who lives far away is a treat, a letter from your favorite relative is a pleasant surprise. But imagine receiving a direct mailer from heaven—from Jehovah God!

The Father really kept a close eye on his early church. He knew these believers were pioneers, with barely a guideline of what a church and/or a Christian should be like. What a sensitive idea he had to send letters to them by way of an apostle! And not only to them, but for us, too. In one fell swoop, God dealt with the unique problems of the first Christians and then preserved those words to benefit all Christians of all times. Fantastic plan!

If you're anything like me, you love to receive mail. Early in our marriage, Jane and I had wars over who picked up the mail at our mailbox. Even junk mail was given careful treatment. Then, one day, she did the unforgivable—she opened an envelope meant for me! It was not addressed to her or even addressed to both of us. It had my name on it, and only mine. I went over the edge. Lucky for me, Jane didn't call the Funny Farm to send up a couple of boys in white coats to fit me for a pretty jacket with wraparound arms. She probably wondered why she married me or at least how I got her to the altar without her learning of my eccentric protectiveness of my mail.

Personally, I thought *she* was way out-of-line. I mean, how on earth could any God-fearing champion of American freedom and justice open someone else's mail? "Don't you know that's a crime?" I hollered, demonstrating just how levelheaded was my approach to Spirit-filled living. "You're a criminal! Do you hear me? A criminal!" My ranting conjured up memories of the man from Gadara who played in the cemetery outside of town, wearing no clothes and rending his flesh against the tombstones. (You can check out that whole story in Mark 5:1–20.)

"Brent," Jane replied, "why are you so upset?" I immediately identified the tone of her mock surprise to be saying, "I know I'm guilty, but I'm going to pretend to be innocent."

I was really beside myself now. "You opened a letter to me that didn't have your name on it, and you want to know why I'm upset!"

"Honey" (she was far too calm for this episode), "it wasn't a letter."

"Oh, yeah," I barked, pointing to the ragged envelope that had fallen victim to her assault. "Then what do you call that?"

"The electric bill."

"What?"

"It's not a letter, it's the electric bill," she said, trying to minimize her felony.

"But it had my name on it!"

"But it's *our* electric bill!"

"But it's addressed to me," I insisted, waving the evidence in front of her face. (See what a Christian example of self-control I can be?)

"Okay. Fine. If you're going to be picky about it. . . ."

I hate it when she ends a discussion like that. So I paid her back in the cutest way. Next time *I* brought in the mail, I opened something addressed to her. (It happened to be an ad for cosmetics.)

My point is, there's good news and bad news about this book. The good news is that it comprises a post office box full of letters to you. Everybody loves mail. Right? The bad news is that several thousand other graduates are reading your mail. Please don't mind sharing. God's Spirit will see to it that each reader finds individual applications. In that way, the letters are personal. That's what makes them belong uniquely to you.

By the way, God's Word is like that to a far greater degree. Millions have read it, for God prepared it for everyone. Yet the Holy Spirit has touched each of us so privately and individually that it is as if the Scriptures were written only to one person—you.

I know you may feel a little funny about having other people reading your mail. But look at it this way: this is not your usual kind of correspondence. Enough said. Here are your letters. . . .

The Declaration of Dependence

Romans

The epistle to the Romans is the true masterpiece of the New Testament and the very purest gospel, which is well worth and deserving that a Christian man should not only learn it by heart, word for word, but also that he should deal with it as the daily bread of men's souls. It can never be too much or too well read or studied, and the more it is handled the more precious it becomes, and the better it tastes.

Martin Luther

1 Access

Through Gates of Splendor

Therefore, since we have been justified through faith, we have peace with God through our Lord Jesus Christ, through whom we have gained access by faith into this grace in which we now stand. And we rejoice in the hope of the glory of God (Rom. 5:1–2).

Dear Graduate,

If you've read through the Old Testament, you know it is filled with strange incidents that a lot of people claim are boring. Though on the surface some of the stuff seems a bit dusty, underneath it can get pretty interesting. And some of it is downright amusing.

The high priest in the Holy of Holies on the Day of Atonement is a perfect example of this. (Check into Leviticus 16 for the whole story). At first glance, all we have is the ritual of a religious man. Boring! But then we notice that here's a guy dressed in rather unusual clothes, making his once-a-year entrance into the sacred sanctum with a long rope tied around his waist. That's curious. He did this on the Day of Atonement to offer a sacrifice for the sins of Israel.

Anyway, going into the Most Holy Place was a big deal. Not just anybody could promenade in there any old time he wanted. Only the high priest could enter, and he could do so only on this special day. That's not all! He had to be clean, properly dressed, and right with God! And what if he wasn't? Well, that's why he wore a rope.

Because if he went behind the curtain into the Most Holy Place and wasn't right with God, or if he messed up his duties—Pow! That was the end of him. And, if that happened, how were the people supposed to get him out? I'll guarantee you nobody else was about to go in there! That's where the rope came in handy. If the priest took an extra long time, or the bells on the bottom of his robe were not ringing, you can imagine his family got a bit nervous.

Why all the fuss about entering into a veiled room? (See how interesting this story has become!) What was in there? Ah, the Ark of the Covenant. And what did the Ark represent? Right—the holy presence of God, and a matter not to be taken lightly. Entering the Holy of Holies, therefore, was symbolic of coming into the very presence of God.

Now you're probably wondering what this has to do with the New Testament. A whole bunch, I promise you. Remember reading in the Gospels about the crucifixion of Jesus Christ? What happened the instant he died? Check out Matthew 27:51: "At that moment the curtain of the temple was torn in two from top to bottom. . . ." Wow! I'll bet that surprised the priests! No man could have ripped the thick fabric of that massive veil. This was an act of God, an act full of meaning.

The torn veil meant free access to God and his mercy. Today we need no priest to offer sacrifices on our behalf; we can come to God directly, through faith in his Son. We have access. The door is always open. And that's what I want to encourage you with in this first letter. If you have trusted Christ, you have the keys to the throne room. The keys are your *knees*! As John Webster wrote:

> Heaven's gates are not so highly arched
> As princes' palaces; they that enter there
> Must go upon their knees.

Odd as it may be, the word *access* is used only three times in the New Testament—all in Paul's letters. Therefore, it seems only appropriate to include it in these letters. It was a special word in Paul's language, and it had unique meanings. Let's pull back the curtain on three of them:

Introduction. "Access" in the long ago referred to the introduction one received when brought before a powerful king. You couldn't just waltz into the king's throne room. First you needed permission, and that was followed by some sort of introduction. Prayer has a similar catch. You have access only if you know the "introducer"— Jesus. Otherwise, you can't get the King to listen. Although it's rude to pray to someone you don't even know, that's no problem for those who know Jesus. He ushers them straight to the throne and says, "Father, this is one of your children who trusted in my name." And the Father bends down his ear to listen very closely.

Haven. An "access" during Paul's day could also refer to the doorway to a quiet place of rest. It was once used to describe the passage a boat took as it entered a peaceful cove. Hey! That's also what prayer is about—rest. Few things settle the soul like time spent talking to God. It's what the writer of Hebrews meant when he penned this part of his letter: "Let us then approach the throne of grace with confidence, so that we may receive mercy and find grace to help us in our time of need" (4:16).

Audience. One of Webster's definitions of "audience" is: "A formal hearing, or the opportunity to be heard." John had this in mind when he wrote: "This is the confidence we have in approaching God: that if we ask anything according to his will, he hears us" (1 John 5:14). That means we can come to God through the name of Jesus and get an instant audience. That's access—coming directly before the throne, right into the Holy of Holies. No waiting. No sacrifices. No curtain. No priest.

Kneeling on my keys,
Brent

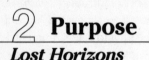 Purpose

Lost Horizons

And we know that in all things God works for the good of those who love him, who have been called according to his purpose (Rom. 8:28).

Dear Graduate,

There you have it: one of the New Testament's most famous verses. Romans 8:28 ranks up there with John 3:16. In fact, a recent poll of pastors shows that John 3 and Romans 8 are the most frequently used sermon texts, and these two verses are by far the most popular. So how could I write to you and not put the great Romans 8:28 right near the beginning?

You know, each time I sit down to write to young people, my memory carries me back. Watch it! I don't have *that* far back to go! Seriously, my senior year seems like a finger snap away. And yet, I've gone through many calendars since then. I was so different those days. Nobody could ever have convinced me then that my life would be as it is today. If ever there was a graduate from the school of Learning Life the Hard Way, it was me. But God chose to bring me the long way around and down a rough road. So many times, in the midst of unusual circumstances, I wondered what on earth was happening to me. All the while, God was working out a plan I could not even imagine.

To have a complete view of life you must be aware that all things are happening according to a divine plan. That is not to say that God chooses evil to occur, although he continues to work out his eternal plan regardless of man's and Satan's pitiful attempts to interrupt him. Isn't that a comforting thought when you're faced with big decisions about your future and what to do with your life? If you will commit your way to the Lord, he will bring it to pass. Just by acknowledging him in all that you do, you can lay hold of God's perfect purpose for your life.

This is what Paul was getting at when he penned the Declaration of Dependence to his Roman readers. What it says is that you're not stuck here on your own. When things are in a mess, you don't have to give up. There's a reason for your troubles. When you think you've lost your way, the Lord is still there right beside you. As you struggle to discover your niche, God is patiently networking the mainframe of his plan. Finally, when you have lost sight of your horizons, God leads you across the wilderness to Jordan and says, "Stick your feet in the water and cross on dry ground into the land of promise, the land of purpose—the land of Providence!"

God doesn't need any help. People who think it necessary to explain every unexplainable puzzle of life make me tired. God doesn't need a lawyer. He can handle himself just fine, so please don't feel as if you must argue on his behalf. Besides, who knows God's eternal plan even half as well as God himself? In fact, who is capable of logic on the ultimate wavelength? Isaiah 55:8–9 ought to simmer down the worriers who fear that God will be misunderstood if someone doesn't defend and interpret his ways in the language of humans. Hit this with your highlighter: "'For my thoughts are not your thoughts, neither are your ways my ways,' declares the LORD. 'As the heavens are higher than the earth, so are my ways higher than your ways and my thoughts than your thoughts.'" Who are we to size up and explain a few problems of mankind when we haven't the slightest idea of God's overall plan? I may not always understand what God is doing, but I know it's always right.

Even sin figures in. Grab hold of your mind; it's about to be boggled. Yes, God is even at work in our failures, which includes our sins! First let's get something straight: God never condones sin. He neither causes it nor encourages it nor takes any pleasure in it whatsoever. Neither does it set well with him when one of his children abuses his grace through habitual, unrestrained sinning. Be sure a paddling is on the way for that. Still, God overrules in our stumblings and brings about good. Take Joseph's brothers the time they played "Let's Make a Deal" with the Midianites. That was outright wickedness. But, despite their grievous wrong against him, listen to Joe's words years later: "'Don't be afraid. Am I in the place of God? You intended to harm me, but God intended it for good to accomplish what is now being done, the saving of many lives'" (Gen. 50:19–20).

You see, God always knows the score. He knew what would happen to Joe and his brothers *before* they were born, and he fit it into his plan. When you think about it, how could God fulfill his purpose without working through sinful man? But we must understand that God works in spite of the sin, not because of it. Even when we blow it, God has something good in store for those of us who love him.

There are no exceptions. "Hold on. Can it be that God is at work in every event?" you ask.

Definitely so!

"Oh, come on!" you argue. "How about when Abel was murdered, when Jacob cheated Esau, or when the Romans crucified Jesus?"

That's right. God was there. No, not promoting these happenings, but just working good. No one—I mean *no one!*—and nothing can prevent God from accomplishing his purposes and plan. What's more, nothing can prevent God from bringing about his best for you—if you want it. Only *you* can ruin your life. And the only way to do that is to stop loving God.

No wonder Romans 8:28 is such a popular verse.

Purposefully,
Brent

3 God's Will

Labyrinth?

*Do not conform any longer to the pattern of this world, but be
transformed by the renewing of your mind. Then you will be
able to test and approve what God's will is—his good,
pleasing, and perfect will* (Rom. 12:2).

Dear Graduate,

Theologians have nearly wrestled the subject of God's will to the
canvas, and I don't want to do that. But how could I leave it out? This
was even big-time stuff to the Bible writers. I mean, nearly everybody got in on the show. Consider the words of these heavy hitters
(the italics are mine, for emphasis):

King David: "Teach me *to do your will,* for you are my God; may
your good Spirit lead me on level ground" (Ps. 143:10).

Isaiah the Prophet: "Yet *it was the Lord's will* to crush him and
cause him to suffer, and though the LORD makes his life a guilt
offering, he will see his offspring and prolong his days, and *the will
of the Lord* will prosper in his hand" (Isa. 53:10).

Jesus Christ: "If anyone *chooses to do God's will,* he will find out
whether my teaching comes from God or whether I speak on my
own" (John 7:17).

Paul the Apostle: "Therefore do not be foolish, but *understand
what the Lord's will is*" (Eph. 5:17).

The Hebrews writer: "God also testified to it by signs, wonders and various miracles, and gifts of the Holy Spirit *distributed according to his will*" (Heb. 2:4).

James: "Instead, you ought to say, '*If it is the Lord's will,* we will live and do this or that'" (James 4:15).

Peter: "As a result, he does not live the rest of his earthly life for evil human desires, *but rather for the will of God*" (1 Peter 4:2).

John: "This is the confidence we have in approaching God: that *if we ask anything according to his will,* he hears us" (1 John 5:14).

That's quite a line-up. No question about it, God's will is a major issue. If we are truly interested in depending upon God, then his will is certain to be paramount in our lives. It won't be mere theory or philosophy or something we simply chat about in Bible study groups. Nor will it be something we trim and tailor to our already-decided ambitions. No way. Anyone who truly plans to follow *God's* plan has no premeditated plan of his own. He (or she) is not slyly fashioning God into the wide collage of a fragmented life. No—the way he follows is the path God leads him to take. He doesn't make up his mind first and then ask God's opinion. Following God's will means making up your mind to do whatever God says, and then asking him what it is. In other words, you really let God be God.

This can be tough to do. It takes humble dedication. It takes wisdom, too. When the waters of decision are murky, a few key questions can help you develop a healthy outlook on the leading of God. Earmark this page for quick future reference. These questions may be useful later.

Does God's will have a bull's-eye? If it does, then the bull's-eye is very big. The Father's will is spacious, never a confining shackle. God's will doesn't make prisoners of his kids. In fact, there's a world of freedom in obeying God. Personally, I believe every Christian can experience "his good, pleasing, and perfect will" by remaining in pursuit of God himself. I am not so sure it is as important to seek God's will as it is to seek God. Everything else gets added as a bonus when you do that (Matt. 6:33). So relax. You don't have to be an archery expert when seeking the guidance of God. Simply aim to know him, and he will hit the bull's-eye *for* you!

What if I had chosen the "other" path? Don't we all wonder that at least once in our lives. Mull this over: What if Moses had refused to lead the children of Israel out of Egypt? What if Jacob hadn't stolen Esau's birthright? What if Absalom had kept David's kingdom for good? What if Judas hadn't betrayed Jesus? First of all, it doesn't make any difference if we speculate, because all of these people did do these things. And, second, even if these events had not occurred, God would have fulfilled his purpose (see "letter 2") anyway. I'm not suggesting that we don't need to carefully weigh our options and pray for God's peace about which to choose. What I mean is that we can't fail God's plan. Still, of course, we want to be in harmony with him.

Where does desire come in? Psalm 37:4 says bluntly, "Delight yourself in the LORD and he will give you the desires of your heart." That has a twofold meaning. Number one: If you delight in God, he creates certain ambitions, goals, dreams—*desires*—and actually places them in your heart. He gives them to you. Number two: As you keep being delighted, he goes about satisfying those desires. He *gives* them to you. That is, he blesses you with them. All along you will want his wants, and it is "his good, pleasing, and perfect will" to give them to you. Go ahead. Pull your "delight" switch, and let God in turn push your "desire" button.

Whatever you do, leave the bows, arrows, and bull's-eyes for the theology buffs.

First things first,
Brent

Letters from the Editor

1 and 2 Corinthians

Paul's relation to the church in Corinth was in some respects peculiar. He was not only the founder of the congregation, but he continued in the closest relation to it. . . . His love for that church was therefore of special intensity. It was analogous to that of a father for a promising son beset with temptations, whose character combined great excellencies with great defects. The epistles to the Corinthians, therefore, reveal to us more of the personal character of the apostle than any of his other letters. They show him to us as a man, as a pastor, as a counselor, as in conflict not only with heretics, but with personal enemies. They reveal his wisdom, his zeal, his forbearance, his liberality of principle and practice in all matters of indifference, his strictness in all matters of right and wrong, his humility, and perhaps above all, his unwearied activity and wonderful endurance.

Charles Hodge

4 Division

Carnal Mathematics

I appeal to you, brothers, in the name of our Lord Jesus Christ, that all of you agree with one another so that there may be no divisions among you and that you may be perfectly united in mind and thought (1 Cor. 1:10).

Dear Graduate,

Christians are sometimes an inglorious bunch. We grumble and feud over silly things, and the world watches on in confusion. What a curious thing it is that we claim to have the answers to life but sometimes act as if we don't know what they are. Now the torch is being passed to you. As you join us in holding forth the example of Christ, it is more important than ever that we raise a standard of unity.

Our society is waiting to see people who make much ado about the Bible learn to live a little of it. As someone has said, "Your talk talks, and your walk talks, but your walk talks louder than your talk talks." Considering the outbreak of letdowns in Christian ministries, one can hardly blame people for adopting the motto of Missourians—"Show me!"

Many times what the world has been shown is how good we are at playing church. Majoring on minors. Fussing. Did you know that some Christians argue about the color of the curtains in the vestibule? One church had a blowout over where the piano belonged.

29

Some wanted it on the right side, others wanted it to stay on the left, where it had been for years. You may not believe this, but the group that wanted the piano on the right came early one Sunday and moved it from the left. The next week, the other group came even earlier and moved it back. Until the mess was finally settled, people were showing up before sunrise to be piano movers. That's playground Christianity.

It's funny, though, that believers do not argue about the important stuff. Everybody's for world evangelism. Nobody's against prayer. And who doesn't want the unchurched to be taught the truth about God's love and forgiveness? Christian folks basically agree on those critical issues; it's the petty nonessentials they gripe about. I wonder how many lost souls have been turned away from God because of divisions and disunity among Christians.

This was a whopper of a problem in the church at Corinth. To be sure, it was at the root of every problem they had. And they had a mega-bunch! What did Paul do about it? He wrote a letter. And it was a hot one, I might add. Sometimes editors get angry letters, but this time the *editor* sent one out himself! As Dad used to say, "They needed some sense knocked into them." *Three* senses, to be exact.

A Sense of Teamwork. The apostle Paul dealt with the division problem throughout his first letter to the Corinthian church, but one of his clearest lectures is in chapter three:

> I planted the seed, Apollos watered it, but God made it grow. So neither he who plants nor he who waters is anything, but only God, who makes things grow. The man who plants and the man who waters have one purpose, and each one will be rewarded according to his own labor. *For we are God's fellow workers.* . . [vv. 6–9, emphasis added].

Did you catch that? Fellow workers! We're on the same team. We're fighting in the same army—no shooting each other down in the trenches!

Jesus taught teamwork, too. Check out Luke 9:49–50, where the disciples are reported to be all shook up over an "outsider" who was exorcising demons in the name of Jesus. "Lord," they may have said as they drew bead on this unnamed servant of God, "this man was slaying devils using your name, and we tried to stop him because he doesn't attend our Bible studies on the Mount of Olives."

Jesus was cool-headed: "Do not stop him, for whoever is not against you is for you" (v. 50). He meant, "Leave him alone." How must our foolish squabbles make Jesus feel?

A Sense of Belongingness. "The body is a unit, though it is made up of many parts; and though all its parts are many, they form one body. So it is with Christ" (1 Cor. 12:12). Paul is saying that we belong to the same body, the church. Wouldn't it be stupid if my right index finger poked out my left eye? Or if my left foot crushed my right one? Or if my teeth intentionally bit off my tongue? "How ridiculous," you're thinking. Well, Christians belong to the same body; yet they do this kind of thing, spiritually speaking, to one another. We need an understanding of what it means to belong to each other. Listen, you may as well learn to accept even the people you love to hate, because you're going to be seeing a lot of them in heaven.

A Sense of Deference. "What's that?" you ask. *Deference* means yielding to the other guy. Thinking of others before we think of ourselves. That, too, was Paul's idea in this letter: "Though I am free and belong to no man, I make myself a slave to everyone, to win as many as possible" (1 Cor. 9:19). In other words, "I don't throw a conniption fit if I don't get my way. It's up to me to control my mind, my mouth, and my moods."

Besides, everyone knows the piano belongs on the right side of the church.

Yours for unity,
Brent

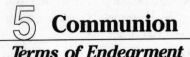 5 Communion

Terms of Endearment

> *For whenever you eat this bread and drink this cup, you proclaim the Lord's death until he comes* (1 Cor. 11:26).

Dear Graduate,

Once upon a time (Don't you just love beginnings like this?), a young man made preparations to go to the foreign mission field and reported at New York headquarters for passage. But he soon realized that the climate at his destination would be unsuitable for his wife's health. Heartbroken, he returned to his home and vowed to make all the money he could, to be used in helping other missionaries. His father, a dentist, had started making unfermented wine as a side business for use in church communion services. The young man decided to take over his father's venture, and he developed it until it grew to vast proportions. His name? If you guessed "Welch," you got it right. And thanks to Mr. Welch's grape juice, thousands of dollars went to the work of missions.

As Paul Harvey would say, "Now you know the *rest* of the story." Except, that isn't the most important part of the story. What is? Well, the part about communion, though I'll bet that's not something you expected to read in a graduation book.

Communion is major big. You see, God ordained only two symbolic rituals for the church: baptism and the Lord's Supper. Baptism represents our *union* with Jesus Christ. When a person is baptized he is saying, "I take my stand with Jesus. My old ways are dead and buried, but he has resurrected me to live a brand-new life." The Lord's Supper represents our *communion* with Jesus. When a believer—and communion is only for believers—participates in communion, he is saying, "Jesus and I are friends. I'm walking in fellowship and harmony with him. His word is cleansing me, his spirit is renewing me day by day, and his grace is sufficient."

Mark this down: you could be dunked in a tank of water a thousand times, with America's ten best preachers praying over you, and it wouldn't give you eternal life. Only Jesus can do that—and he will if you trust in him by faith. Also, you could gobble down five loaves of communion bread and gulp down a gallon of sacred Welch's (given to you directly by Billy Graham himself), but that wouldn't give you eternal life either. Baptism and communion are for people who know the Lord, not for people for whom he is a stranger. These acts aren't even to be practiced by people who merely *wish* to know the Lord.

Please don't get me wrong. These two ordinances are precious to our Savior, but they belong solely to Christians and are so important that Paul wrote about them frequently. In fact, he dedicated a whole section of his first letter to the Corinthians to the practice of communion (1 Cor. 11:17–34). He told us three things to remember when we dine in memory of Christ's sacrifice for us at Golgotha:

1. *Communion is a sacred event.* "For whenever you eat this bread and drink this cup, you proclaim the Lord's death until he comes" (1 Cor. 11:26). Communion is a special time for remembering Jesus and thus is to be treated with reverence. I don't mean we should make a nervous ritual out of it. On the other hand, we must be careful not to reduce the Lord's Supper to a boring and meaningless routine. Personally, that's why I'm not fond of having communion in church every week. I think it should be a special time. Familiarity takes the edge off, in my opinion. Still, Paul's point was: keep it holy.

2. ***Communion is a solemn event.*** "Therefore, whoever eats the bread or drinks the cup of the Lord in an unworthy manner will be guilty of sinning against the body and blood of the Lord" (1 Cor. 11:27). If that isn't a solemn thought, nothing is. By the way, what does Paul mean by "an unworthy manner"? He certainly doesn't mean accidental spilling of the juice. Proper etiquette is a nice touch, but God doesn't have Emily Post watching over our table manners. Paul was referring to people with gross, unconfessed sin in their lives who partake of communion anyway. That should be unthinkable.

3. ***Communion is a searching event.*** Paul also told the Corinthians: "A man ought to examine himself before he eats of the bread and drinks of the cup" (1 Cor. 11:28). Remember, this is all about fellowship with God. The person who is walking in harmony with God can enjoy the communion supper—with its terms of endearment—because of remembering what Jesus did on the cross. But the person living contrary to God's will has no real appreciation for what communion represents and should pray instead of eat. When the Lord's Supper is over, all who participated as ordained should have a clean heart and a clear conscience before God. And the images of Calvary will be etched upon their minds with renewed clarity.

God smiles on that. So does Mr. Welch.

Come and dine,
Brent

 Comfort

Stand by Me

If we are distressed, it is for your comfort and salvation; if we are comforted, it is for your comfort, which produces in you patient endurance of the same sufferings we suffer (2 Cor. 1:6).

Dear Graduate,

Not too long ago I read about two young men who had served together in World War I and had been friends for their entire lifetimes. They had played together, gone to the same school, participated in the same sports, and finally enlisted in the army together. God's providence determined that they eventually would be in the same area of battle together.

After rugged and bitter combat one day, it was found that one of the young soldiers was missing somewhere out in what the troops called "No Man's Land." The other boy, safe and unhurt, went to his commanding officer to request permission to go out and look for his friend. He was told that it was no use, since no one could be alive out there after so many hours of fighting and shelling. But the young man insisted and was finally given permission to go.

A few hours later he came into the camp carrying the limp, dead body of his friend over his shoulder. The commanding officer saw him and said, "Didn't I tell you it was useless to go?" And the youth replied through tears, but with a gentle radiance, "But it was not useless. I got there in time to hear him whisper, 'I knew you'd come.'"

This story reminds me of a series of messages I recently preached in our church entitled, "Healing Wounded Soldiers." You see, we are *all* soldiers. Paul teaches us that in one of his other letters: "Endure hardship with us like a good soldier of Christ Jesus" (2 Tim. 2:3).

In 2 Corinthians 10:3–4, Paul further describes our role as soldiers:

> For though we live in the world, we do not wage war as the world does. The weapons we fight with are not the weapons of the world. On the contrary, they have divine power to demolish strongholds.

We have the weapons of prayer, the Word of God, which is the sword of the Spirit, and the whole armor of God. We're not a namby-pamby army. God has equipped us with all we need to nuke the devil.

Unfortunately, some of our own soldiers get hit in the midst of the battle. That's what Paul was referring to when he wrote to the Corinthians about suffering. Wounds are painful. They sometimes heal slowly and often leave scars. But listen, getting wounded is just part of being a soldier. If you plan to be a faithful disciple, don't be surprised if a few shots come your way. Actually, more than a few! And if you get hit, don't let yourself give up. Simply store this chapter in your first-aid kit and pull it out when the pain sets in. Here are the bandages—words of wisdom for the wounded:

Weakness is better than strength. Before Paul closed his last letter to the Corinthians, he penned these words:

> To keep me from becoming conceited because of these surpassingly great revelations, there was given me a thorn in my flesh [*Did you hear that? A wound!*], a messenger of Satan, to torment me. Three times I pleaded with the Lord to take it away from me. But he said to me, "My grace is sufficient for you, for my power is made perfect in

weakness." Therefore I will boast all the more gladly in my weaknesses, so that Christ's power may rest on me. That is why, for Christ's sake, I delight in weaknesses, in insults, in hardships, in persecutions, in difficulties. For when I am weak, then I am strong [2 Cor. 12:7–10].

Whoa! Amazing! Paul learned to live with his wounds, and he didn't leave the front lines. He stayed in the trenches. That's maturity. That's bravery and real heroism. True soldiering.

Too much pain indicates too much "self." Upon another occasion Paul wrote these words: "I have been crucified with Christ and I no longer live, but Christ lives in me. The life I live in the body, I live by faith in the Son of God, who loved me and gave himself for me" (Gal. 2:20). Once crucified with Christ, our old life is over and we should feel no pain. If we feel pain, we have forgotten that our former ways are no more. It means we are still in this body—we are not yet perfect. But if the pain is overwhelming, too much of the old self is still alive. This makes me wonder if God sometimes allows us to get wounded just so "self" can be put out of the way. Ouch! That's a little like disinfectant on a cut, isn't it?

Wounding is necessary to glory. Paul explained this very well: "For it has been granted to you on behalf of Christ not only to believe on him, but also to suffer for him" (Phil. 1:29). The Purple Heart isn't given to a soldier who has no scratches. And we must not forget that Jesus was *wounded* for our transgressions and bruised for our iniquities. If we suffer with him, we reign with him. In other words, those who have never suffered were never soldiers in the Lord's army. Never having gone to battle, they never actually became disciples. You know what else that means? When Jesus comes to comfort his wounded, those other people never get to whisper, "I knew you'd come."

Save the wounded,
Brent

Church Newsletters

Galatians; Ephesians; Philippians; Colossians

[*Galatians:*] *It is doubtful whether any letter has stirred up more controversy and at the same time has affected more decisively the estimate that men have formed of the Christianity of the New Testament. . . . During the past century no writing of Paul has been more of a battleground in the debate concerning the meaning of Paul and the precise place he occupied in early Christianity.*

Ned G. Stonehouse

[*Ephesians:*] *There are passages in this first chapter, especially towards its end, where the Apostle is carried out above and beyond himself, and loses and abandons himself in a great outburst of worship and praise and thanksgiving. I repeat, therefore, that there is nothing more sublime in the whole range of Scripture than this Epistle to the Ephesians.*

Martin Lloyd-Jones

[Philippians:] It is a simple letter to personal friends. It has no theological discussions and no rigid outline and no formal development. It rambles along just as any real letter would with personal news and personal feelings and outbursts of personal affection between tried friends.

Doremus Hayes

[Colossians:] I have a feeling that we would have revival in our churches if all true believers dare to live what Colossians teaches.

Warren Wiersbe

7 Corruption

Little Shop of Horrors

"A little yeast works through the whole batch of dough"
(Gal. 5:9).

Dear Graduate,

I love golf. I love to watch it, play it, and talk about it. I love the equipment. I even think the concept is marvelous: hit a little bitty ball hundreds of yards with a long shining stick and try to get it into a little bitty hole. Probably my favorite moment in a golf round—outside of sinking an "impossible" putt—is hitting a perfect shot out of the fairway and watching it land on the green.

When a mishandled club chops out some turf, that's a divot. And when a long shot lands solidly on the green, it can leave a ball mark. Golf courses are designed with a special type of grass that is very durable, but divots can cause fairway pock marks—and hard-hit approach shots can damage the green—if they aren't "fixed" by the golfers as they play. If left to heal themselves, these scars can make a course look like a zit-faced teenager—blemishes everywhere. Yet most of them can be quickly and easily repaired by lifting out the ball indentation with a tee or using a divot-repair prong.

The other day when I was taking a Coke break in the clubhouse, I read a little sign that had this reminder to golfers:

> A new ball mark repaired by a player takes
> FIVE SECONDS
> A freshly repaired ball mark will completely heal in
> TWENTY-FOUR HOURS
> A fresh ball mark left unrepaired for only one hour requires
> FIFTEEN HOURS' TIME
> Before the ugly scar has satisfactorily healed
> PLEASE REPAIR ALL BALL MARKS
> AND DIVOTS

There's a lot of spiritual truth in that sign. When ball marks are tended to immediately, they heal quickly; but those left alone worsen and spoil the playing field for others. Sin is like that, too. If we deal with sin in our lives right away, minimum damage is done and our fellowship with God is quickly restored. If ignored, sin will grow and spread and corrupt our whole personality.

Now you have the gist of Paul's verse to the Galatians. As sure as a small amount of yeast works through a whole batch of dough, it only takes a little to corrupt a lot. The defiled can easily ruin the pure. The filthy can suddenly overwhelm the clean. The rotten can smell up the fragrant in a moment. Little chips light great fires. Small differences abound into great discords. That which is evil is soon learned. To sum up, as it has been aptly spoken: "All it takes for evil to triumph over good is for the good to do nothing."

Oops! Pardon me. I'm up on my soapbox again. Sorry about that, but this subject really gets me worked up. Our society has gradually become so accustomed to dabbling with immorality and corruption that it doesn't realize how subtle its seduction has been. The cultural changes begun so innocently two decades ago have gradually saturated American thinking. And many years before this moral (Or should I say "immoral"?) revolution started, the groundwork was being laid. Now look how a smidgen of yeast has perverted a society's standards!

Paul was using yeast symbolically to get across his point, and I think he had a few specifics in mind when he wrote this. I think he purposely used the yeast analogy to hint at some of the hidden traps we may accidentally step into if we're careless.

False Doctrine. "'Be careful,' Jesus said to them. 'Be on your guard against the yeast of the Pharisees and Sadducees'" (Matt. 16:6). What did Jesus mean? The disciples seemed to be so dumb sometimes. Here they thought Jesus was simply mad at them for not bringing bread for their trip. Brilliant! However, a few verses later we read that they finally understood that Jesus meant false teaching—the yeast represented false doctrine.

Get the message? I can't warn you loud enough about cults and religiosity. Beware! They will spoil you if you fool with them. Don't have Bible studies with Jehovah's Witnesses or Mormons. Look out for Eastern Mysticism, too. And don't fall for people's ideas just because they speak your lingo. Be sure every doctrine you hear can be proven with the Scriptures. False doctrine is a dangerous yeast.

Seductive Ideas. 2 Peter 2:14 tells us that "the unstable" are the ones who get seduced. And James 1:8 tells us that the unstable are those who are "double-minded." What we have here are spiritual schizophrenics. The polluted ideas of our culture can easily corrupt those who cannot make up their minds whether or not to live for God.

The Bible records that Daniel determined in his heart not to be defiled by the king's "food and wine" (see Dan. 1:8). He had his mind made up ahead of time and didn't sway back and forth between two opinions like a monkey swinging on a trapeze. His heart was set. Seduction is a slow-moving yeast that seeks to "immoralize" the weak. Be unstable for long and you'll be its victim.

Evil Influences. We've already taken a bird's-eye view of Paul's letters to the Corinthians, but he often said things in his writing that overlap. For example, in 1 Corinthians 5:7 he mentioned the yeast ordeal to them, and then later (in 12:2) reminded the Corinthians of how they were once led astray to worship idols by evil influences. What a critical truth: bad friends corrupt good morals. The wrong company can carry a yeast of destruction. Although we can't cut

43

ourselves off from mankind, and "hermit religion" is not God's idea of theology, we must be constantly alert to how we're being influenced by various circumstances and individuals.

Especially watch out for golf nuts!

Fix your ball marks and divots,
Brent

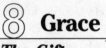 # Grace

The Gift

For it is by grace you have been saved, through faith—and this not from yourselves, it is the gift of God—not by works, so that no one can boast (Eph. 2:8–9).

Dear Graduate,

The famous nineteenth-century preacher Charles Spurgeon told the story of a minister who went to call upon a poor woman, intending to give her some money and other help because he knew she was very poor. With his money in hand he knocked at her door, but she did not answer. He figured she was not home, so he returned to his study. Later he met her at the church and told her he had remembered her need: "I dropped by your house and knocked several times. You must not have been home."

"When did you come by?" she asked.

"At about noon."

"Oh, my!" The woman covered her mouth with her hand as she added, "I heard you and I'm so sorry I didn't answer, but I thought it was the landlord calling for the rent."

It is so vital that you hear me on this next point. It is a matter of eternity. The gospel is not God's way of calling for the rent. And I'm not calling for the rent either. If you've read this far, you have heard some tough talk. Maybe you think I've been too pushy, or that being a Christian is too much of an ordeal. Actually, I don't know what you think. But I certainly don't want to give the impression that I'm being super-negative and just trying to tell you your duty.

Some of the sayings in my first seven letters have been hard to hear, and I can guarantee you that after this one I'll quite likely pick up where I left off. But *this* letter is positive, and it's the heart and soul of God's truth. This subject is God's favorite. In fact, it is the cornerstone of Bible teaching.

What you're about to hear is "the old, old story," as the hymn goes. It is irreplaceable. It is impeccable. It is endearing. The central idea is that God hasn't come to call for the rent; he has come to pay it himself! He isn't interested in us for what duties we can perform; he simply loves us—with an infinite, incomprehensible, incomparable love! Jesus stands at your door and knocks, and he hasn't come to collect. He truly seeks to enter into a covenant of friendship with you. And while there is some cost in following him, he promises to pay that, too.

Grace—that is the lifeblood of the gospel. It is the heartbeat of God's love for us. What wonder! If I can, let me telescope the beauty of grace with these scattered thoughts:

What is grace? Paul answered this question in such a touching, reflective way in his second letter to the Corinthians: "For you know the grace of our Lord Jesus Christ, that though he was rich, yet for your sakes he became poor, so that you through his poverty might become rich" (2 Cor. 8:9). Though spiritually we were poor, miserable, wretched bums, Jesus sped across the galaxy and one night put aside all that was glorious and became a Savior who was born to die. Jesus had rescue on his mind. For every up-and-comer and every down-and-outer, he paid the ultimate sacrifice. Now he says, "Come to me if you're burdened with sin's heavy weight. When you finally awaken to the unpayable price, call out to me and I'll give you rest" (Matt. 11:28–30, the Earles Paraphrase). God's riches at Christ's expense—that's what grace is. Do you want true riches? Become a Son-worshiper!

Grace is a growing matter. Peter said: "But grow in the grace and knowledge of our Lord and Savior Jesus Christ. . ." (2 Peter 3:18). Grace doesn't stop at salvation; it's a lifetime deal. God's maximum love keeps on even in our worst of times. As children in the Lord we keep growing, while grace steadies the metabolism of our spiritual lives. When you dig into the Book and devote yourself to prayer and surrender in obedience to the Savior, grace is at work. Here's the point: we can't do any or enough good works to convince God to save us. Neither can we do enough to become his special buddies *after* we're saved. Grace is spelled G-I-F-T. God gives us the gift of eternal life, but the gift of growth, too.

Grace is a necessity of life. "How can I live through my pain?" we sometimes ask ourselves. "How will I face this? How will I recover? Will life ever be the same again?" Surely we've all been through this depth of emotional agony at one time or another. But the Christian has a unique asset. You guessed it: grace. Yes, God shines his unmerited favor on his kids. No, we don't deserve it. We're absolutely unworthy. Still, at our darkest hour, he gives us a gift that brings the courage to carry on. ". . .'God opposes the proud but gives grace to the humble'" (James 4:6).

And through all of this, he never once comes to collect the rent.

Grace to you,
Brent

⑨ Single-Mindedness

Magnificent Obsession

. . . But one thing I do: Forgetting what is behind and straining toward what is ahead, I press on toward the goal to win the prize for which God has called me heavenward in Christ Jesus (Phil. 3:13–14).

Set your minds on things above, not on earthly things (Col. 3:2).

Dear Graduate,

Specialize! We have enough many-faceted and versatile Christians. What we need is a generation of "one thing" Christians. The core of single-mindedness is found in Paul's "one-thing-I-do" mentality. The need for this kind of thinking is an important truth taught throughout the Scriptures. The psalmist was a single-minded man, sturdy in all his ways. His testimony? "*One thing* I ask of the LORD, this is what I seek: that I may dwell in the house of the LORD all the days of my life. . ." (Ps. 27:4, emphasis added). And remember the wealthy young ruler who came to Jesus seeking eternal life? Jesus told him that he lacked *one thing*: a willingness to surrender all of himself—even his money (Mark 10:21). Hard-working Martha was rebuked by Jesus when she worried about the distractions of preparing a big meal and was upset at her sister Mary's failure to pitch in and help. He taught her that only *one thing* was needed (Luke 10:42).

We're an easily distracted society. And culture-taught frenzy has crept into the lives of too many Christians. They want to be model disciples, corporate successes, dedicated political supporters, community chieftains, competent Bible-study captains, or school-board presidents or PTA chairmen or scout leaders, and well-liked neighbors. Don't misunderstand me. I'm not saying these things aren't important, nor suggesting that everyone should bug out and turn lazy. Several somebodies need to do these jobs. And there's no reason why a Christian can't participate. Here's my point, and I think it was Paul's too: *Every detail and task of life must be channeled through our single purpose—to walk humbly with our God.* All other attractions can become *dis*-tractions if we do not maintain this as our top priority. If we do not have a single mind about our relationship with God, being a Christian will be only a part of our lives, only a piece of who and what we are. But it should describe *all* of our doings.

The verses in this letter's heading tell us three things involved in single-minded thinking:

Forgetting. Paul refused to dwell on past failures or successes. He forced them out of his thoughts. He disciplined his mind to disallow both yesterday's "bombs" and the bounties that might carry him through today. Every day brought forth fresh fruit in his life. Runners who turn to look back lose speed, so smart runners fix their eyes on the finish line. This is what makes a true champion for Christ. Which one of us couldn't do with more mental conditioning? Surely none of us can honestly say, "I never have problems with thoughts of yesterday's mountaintops or of last week's valleys. I'm always—one hundred percent of the time—on top of my thoughts." Obviously, we could all stand a little sifting of our brainwaves.

Setting. Colossians 3:2 mentions the importance of mind-set.

Here's an amplified paraphrase of what the number one New Testament letter writer was saying: "Let heaven flood into your mind. Let heavenly things overflow your thoughts. Be absorbed in the cares of eternity. Be consumed with what matters forever, not with what lasts for only a while." Runners who play to the crowd rarely win, because grandstanders are too self-absorbed. They have yet to set their minds on a single goal. That is the *one thing* many of this year's graduates lack. Why not accept the challenge of fixing your mind and heart on the singular goal of pleasing God? Not for the sake of what others may say. Not for the goal of mere success. Not for meaningless feelings of being "religious." Not even for the blessings it will bring to you. But simply to bring joy to the heart of God, your Creator. Set your affection dial correctly and you'll tune in the right stuff.

Straining. Now we're talking real athletics. Although Paul strained toward the mark of God's will for his life, I'm afraid too many of today's Christians just don't have this kind of motivation. No push. No inner drive. They don't try hard enough. C. H. Spurgeon's "John Ploughman" penned this little ditty on trying:

> Once let every man say "Try,"
> Very few on straw would lie;
> Fewer still of want would die;
> Pans would all have fish to fry;
> Pigs would fill the poor man's sty;
> Want would cease and need would fly;
> Wives and children cease to cry;
> Poor rates would not swell so high
> Things wouldn't go so much awry—
> You'd be glad, and so would I.

Nehemiah rebuilt Jerusalem's wall with this philosophy. He showed his single-mindedness one day when a couple of ambushers tried to lure him away from the site. He sent them this message: ". . .'I am carrying on a great project and cannot go down. Why should the work stop while I leave it and go down to you?' Four times they sent me the same message, and each time I gave them the same answer" (Neh. 6:3–4).

He had a one-track mind—single-mindedness!

See you on the wall,
Brent

High Notes
1 and 2 Thessalonians

In my review of the dates of writing of the books of the New Testament, I found that the apostle's letters to the Thessalonicans were written in the year A.D. 50, about 15 years after his conversion and less than 20 years after the crucifixion of Jesus. The more I reread these Epistles, the more I felt I was in touch with "pure Paul" before his writing style was perfected. The early date of their writing made them all the more attractive and vital. The unstudied, personal impact of the letters read less like a treatise and more like a personal friend's urgent response to authentic spiritual need in living life as it was meant to be.

Lloyd John Ogilvie

10 Motives

A Question of Balance

*For the appeal we make does not spring from error or
impure motives, nor are we trying to trick you* (1 Thess. 2:3).

Dear Graduate,

What makes us do the things we do? What moves us? What
inspires us? Motives. Right? Problem: What happens when the
motives get mixed? Like the little girl Keith Miller tells about in
Habitation of Dragons. The child wrote home from summer camp to
explain her dilemma and seek advice:

> Mommy, I'm not sure if I am being nice to these people because I like
> them or because I believe it will make them think I'm a neat kid. And
> it worries me. Should I quit being so friendly?

I have often wrestled with the dragon of mixed motives. It's hard
for me to admit this, but sometimes I've walked to the opening of a
Sunday worship service wondering about my motives. Was I going
there to preach a good sermon so that people would think I was
eloquent? Or was I going because I wanted to tell needy people the
good news as God's unworthy ambassador? I have at once struggled
with two motives pushing me to do a good thing. Deep within my
heart I want God to be pleased, but there have been times when I so
hated my ego's longings to be complimented that I nearly turned

around and walked away from the pulpit. Talk about all-star wrestling! Somehow, once I get started sharing God's Word, I forget about the motives and just enjoy spreading the good news. But, afterwards, it's back into the ring for more body-smashing soul searching.

Maybe that's why Frederick Buechner's words from *The Magnificent Defeat* are so meaningful to me:

> The voice that we hear over our shoulders never says, "First be sure that your motives are pure and selfless and then follow me." If it did, then we could none of us follow. So when later the voice says, "Take up your cross and follow me," at least part of what is meant by "cross" is our realization that we are seldom any less than nine parts fake. Yet our feet can insist on answering him anyway, and on we go, step after step, mile after mile. How far? How far?

The "M's" of motivation hold some wise insight into the feelings that make us tick as humans. You may want to keep them handy for the next time your motives turn upside down and play Humpty Dumpty. Fortunately, the puzzle can be put back together again.

Masking. How good we are at putting up a front! Aren't we skillful at pretending we're doing something for one reason when we're really doing it for another? But Paul told the Thessalonians, "Hey, look. We have been real with you. No masks. No faking. No error. What you see is what you get." That's more than a lot of ministries can claim these days! Paul never used a God-is-going-to-take-me-home threat. And he didn't have to worry about having an illicit incident from his past make headlines in *The Thessalonian Enquirer*. Paul didn't put on a show. No, he wasn't perfect. He often sinned and failed. But he didn't put up a pretense. Although many different things motivated him, Paul never had to wear a mask to hide anything from the people who trusted him.

Manipulating. "We haven't tried to trick you," the apostle promised them. Paul didn't yank people around with his cunning communication abilities. He could have, you know, since he was a brilliant speaker and writer. How easy it would have been for him to dominate people if his motives had been impure. Too many Christians have this bad blood in their veins. They have mastered the skill of getting their way, and they can and do sweet-talk the naive into following along. In the Old Testament, Jacob is a perfect example of this. He finagled Esau out of the birthright with something as worthless as a bowl of soup. Shrewd Jake could probably sell the Communists on democracy if he were alive today. So, not only must we beware of faking to cover up our real intentions, we must guard against trying to use our talents and influence to control others. Especially when our desires are questionable.

Misunderstanding. Mark this down: no matter how sincere your motives, someone will criticize you. Don't be surprised when it happens. Jesus had perfect motives at all times, yet he was misjudged often. If he healed a cripple on the Sabbath, he could count on somebody to say, "The only reason he did that was to break the law. He just wants to stir up the people to rebellion." Of course, that was a stupid and farfetched accusation. But that kind of junk is typical of people who have a sour outlook on life. Only you and God are certain about your motives. And a lot of time you can't be too sure about yourself. Don't worry, though. It's pretty normal to be fighting mixed motives.

The only time you need to worry about your motivational balance is when you're tempted to break out the masquerade costumes and hide your true self. Masks and manipulation are straight from the dragon's lair.

Find a balance,
Brent

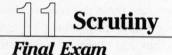 **Scrutiny**

Final Exam

Test everything. Hold on to the good. (1 Thess. 5:21).

Dear Graduate,
Get ready for some questions:

1. Where will you be in ten years? What will you be doing?
2. How will you get there?
3. Do you have plans in the next six months that will get you underway to reach your goal?
4. Have you considered what may sidetrack you?
5. Have you written down some of your plans in order to evaluate your progress later on?
6. *Have you taken the utmost of care to consult God's will first of all?*

That last question is really the most important one. And though God may not be saying "Yes" or "No" to your particular desires at the moment, passing this "test" means you have verified your commitment to obey him if somewhere down the road he guides you differently than you had planned. Have you determined to remain willing and flexible to change according to the leading that God's Spirit may give?

Tougher than any exam you have taken in a school course is your lifelong testing, the system of checks and balances you will use to determine your values. Some of the things you count precious today may not be at all important to you five years from now. Your "tests" will be checkpoints that show what influences your changes. Some things that are vaguely important to your values today may become absolutely vital in the next five years. How carefully you test everything will determine how well you lay the bricks as you construct your life. If you have no tests, no means of scrutinizing what's really important, you will quite likely build a shoddy foundation that will collapse under the least extra strain.

Some time ago I dropped by a trailer home where one of the teenagers who had occasionally visited our church was known to hang out. He had been hard to track down, but his mom suggested that I look for him there. A young man in his mid-twenties invited me in, then went to get the teen I had come to see. Evidently he was asleep in one of the bedrooms. During the several minutes while I sat waiting, I casually glanced around the living room. I was at first surprised to find *Marijuana Grower's Guide* lying on the coffee table. Being familiar with the drug culture from my B.C. days (Before Christ), I thumbed curiously through the book. Then it dawned on me that I was surrounded by a room full of plants—marijuana plants! This guy was obviously a drug dealer. The more I looked around, the more signs I saw: books and magazines on various drugs and their use, drug paraphernalia, "roaches" from used-up "joints" in the ash tray, Baggies here and there containing pot, pills, and other potpourri.

Rage fell over me—then fear for the teenager, who was no doubt being influenced by all this. Then I remembered what it is like to be lost and apart from Jesus Christ. How could I expect goodness from a person who obviously had never tasted grace? I wondered how this man, then approaching some of the prime years of his life, ever got wrapped up in that scene. Did he *plan* to become that way? Eight or ten years ago, fresh out of school, was that his goal? I couldn't believe that it was.

No, I'm sure it wasn't. What I discerned that day is something I have many times since confirmed in my own mind, in many other similar situations. People get into the worst of circumstances because they have no iron-clad plans. As they begin to go with the flow, what happens is that their values get washed away. Soon, nothing matters. Everything seems wasted. They feel as if there's no turning back. Suddenly, they're hooked, addicted, trapped, defeated, and indifferent. They never planned for things to turn out that way. They just never planned at all.

This is how a naive young girl eventually gets swept into prostitution. This is how curious college students get addicted to cocaine. This is how unsuspecting teenagers become homosexuals. This is how thieves, bums, and losers become what they are. It's not that they planned it that way. They just didn't plan it *not to be* that way. No tests. No measures. Therefore, no values. And, if no values, then no stoppers. No restraints.

What Paul was saying here was, "Scrutinize. Test everything. And wrap your arms around the good. Never let go." *Question:* How do you "test" things?

Write out your values. Sure, I know this will take some time. But if you don't care enough to invest some time in charting your values, then how in the world do you expect to know what is good enough to hold on to? Go ahead. Find a sheet of paper. I'll wait. . . .

Back? Good. Write this across the top of the page: "Lord, what's really important?" Write today's date, then begin listing the things you consider valuable in life. Here are some ideas to mull over. But add your own. And be thorough.

What is going to be your role in your family in the years to come? What kind of family do you want to have when you get married?

How do you feel about marriage? Children? Love? Romance? Sex? Divorce? Child-rearing? Discipline? Education? Family ties?

What are your goals in life? Spiritual? Intellectual? Emotional? Physical? Vocational? Relationship-wise?

Do you have specific beliefs about friendship?

How do you plan to handle failures, setbacks, and disappointments?
What place will money and material things have in your life?
Where does God fit in? *Does* he? Do you fit into his plans?
Where do you want to be in ten years? Doing what?

Now keep your list somewhere handy. Refer to it frequently. Modify it. Add Scripture references. Every year do a major revision—holding on to the good.

Never burn bridges. You never know when you may need someone or something from your past. Good can be learned from even the bad. If one day you need to backtrack to find out where you lost your way, you may need an old friend, your parents, a grandma, a former youth pastor or schoolteacher. Don't burn your bridges! They are your link to the past. And sometimes they are the bread crumbs to be used in finding your way back to what's really important.

Check back with me in ten years and let me know how you're doing. That will be the real final exam.

Walk wisely,
Brent

12 Prophecy

Back to the Future

Concerning the coming of our Lord Jesus Christ and our being gathered to him, we ask you, brothers, not to become easily unsettled or alarmed by some prophecy, report or letter supposed to have come from us, saying that the day of the Lord has already come (2 Thess. 2:1–2).

Dear Graduate,

Jesus may return to the earth in your lifetime and mine. Imagine that! King Jesus riding out of heaven on a cloud, lowering himself into our world once again. Except the next time Jesus steps foot on our planet, everyone will know who he is. He won't arrive as a baby in Bethlehem the next time; he will be the commander of God's angels, perhaps astride a white horse.

Late-breaking news: there is a lot of disagreement over details of the end times. Yes, Bible scholars have formed scads of viewpoints on what will happen when the end begins to set in. But I don't want to bore you with all that rigamarole and arguing. Instead, let me sketch out some unchanging truths about the prophecy of Jesus' return. This was heavy-duty stuff with Paul. In fact, he mentioned it in every chapter of both letters to the Thessalonians except the last one. (Check out 1 Thess. 1:10, 2:19, 3:13, 4:16, 5:2 and 23; 2 Thess. 1:7–10, 2:1.) Now for Paul's reminders concerning *the* Event of events:

It is sure. "For the Lord himself will come down from heaven. . ." (1 Thess. 4:16). Whatever else you believe about the prophecy of Jesus' coming, believe this: it is certain. Make no doubt about it. As surely as he came the first time, he's coming again. Remember how, several days after the resurrection, the Lord floated off into heaven? The disciples just stood there with their mouths hanging open. Two angels instantly appeared to speak with them: "'Men of Galilee,' they said, 'why do you stand here looking into the sky? This same Jesus, who has been taken from you into heaven, will come back in the same way you have seen him go into heaven'" (Acts 1:11). Horoscope readers, astrologers, and fortune-tellers only try to predict future events. But God *promises* his predictions and then always does just what he said he would do. Jesus is coming! Are you ready?

It is going to be sudden. ". . . you know very well that the day of the Lord will come like a thief in the night (1 Thess. 5:2). One second, peace and quiet. Then, Kaboom! Sudden destruction. I believe in what is called "the imminent return" of Jesus. That means he could come for his followers at any moment. In other words, nothing special has to happen before Jesus arrives and says, "Come here." That's when every true believer is going home. How long will that take? First Corinthians 15:52 says it will be "in a flash, in the twinkling of an eye. . . ." The word *twinkling* in Paul's letter meant the smallest-known segment of time to the minds of his readers. How long would that be for us? A millisecond? We're talking *sudden*! One twinkle, there's earth. Poof! The next twinkle, there's heaven.

It is going to be separating. "But you, brothers, are not in darkness so that this day should surprise you like a thief (1 Thess. 5:4). An undeniable part of this prophecy is that those who do not receive the truth will not join Jesus at his coming. They will be judged and *separated* from him for an eternity. This is tough stuff. Listen, if your best friend is a Christian and you're not, you will be separated from the friend when Jesus comes. If you have trusted

Jesus but have a family member who has not, you will be separated when the Lord returns. The end of the world is a time of judgment.

Those basic truths about the end times ought to provoke at least three things in our hearts:

1. A desire to be right with God, to be ready to meet Jesus when he comes back.
2. A motivation to live life to its fullest and to the glory of God, so that we don't squander and waste the precious gift God has given us—the gift of life.
3. A burden to share with others the love and forgiveness of God before time runs out.

No biblical prophecy is meant to be a deciphering problem. Too many people are wrapped up in breaking a code and calculating dates. Paul didn't write about the day of the Lord for *that* purpose, and he didn't know that today's Christians would go seminar crazy over this prophecy. He wrote about the second coming so as to comfort and inspire. The problem with a lot of Christians is not that they need to learn more about future events but that they are so lost in the future that they need to get back to the present. Think about it! For the day is at hand.

See you in the air?

Send in the clouds,
Brent

Lectures to My Students

1 and 2 Timothy; Titus

The First and Second Epistles to Timothy, and the Epistle to Titus form a distinct group among the letters written by Paul, and are now known as the Pastoral Epistles because they were addressed to two Christian ministers . . . . In each of them, however, there is a great deal more than is covered or implied by the designation "Pastoral"—much that is personal, and much also that is concerned with Christian faith and doctrine and practice generally.

John Rutherford

 # 13 **Doctrine**

The Torch We Pass

*Watch your life and doctrine closely. Persevere in them,
because if you do, you save both yourself and your hearers*
(1 Tim. 4:16).

Dear Graduate:

I laugh almost every time I read the story one preacher re-
counted of the words spoken to him by an elderly woman, one
Sunday after he had delivered the evening sermon. She said: "Pastor,
I really like your preachin', 'cause you don't talk about no doctrine
or nothin'." That smacks my funny bone because doctrine must be
at the heart of everything we teach. If a preacher preaches "no
doctrine," he preaches "nothin'," all right. The very word *doctrine*
means "teaching." As hard as it may be to believe, every week in
hundreds of pulpits are so-called ministers who stand up and fritter
away thirty minutes of good time saying next to nothing, without so
much as a shred of doctrine in their sermons. I recently heard of a
pastor who spoke to a huge congregation on the subject of "the
most distinguished animal in God's kingdom"—the rooster. He told
the people the rooster was distinguished because he "looks toward
heaven when he crows." Now, if that doesn't beat all other efforts to
trivialize Scripture!

Doctrine scares some people because it can be heavy-duty stuff.

Enough confusing doctrinal questions have been asked to start a million theological debates. And the average Christian couldn't care less about what the answers are. In some cases, I doubt God cares either! Consider these age-old questions, for instance:

Can God create a rock so heavy he can't lift it?
How many angels can fit on the head of a pin?
When Jesus died, did he shed every drop of his blood?
Just how lost is man? How sinful? How depraved?
    [Come on! I mean—good grief!—how lost is lost?]
Which came first, the chicken or the egg?
What is the difference between the spirit and the soul?
Does God love Satan?

The list could go on, but I think you have the gist of the idea. Some of these questions may make for an interesting rap session, but that's about as far as it goes. Unfortunately, this is the concept some people have about all doctrine. To them, "doctrine" is a bunch of blab that seminarians argue about. They have been given the impression that doctrine is boring. No fizz. No snap, crackle, or pop—so it's for dullards. Most of these false notions have been caused by poor teaching and meaningless debates. The result? Today we have a generation of Christians who know very little about what they believe or, at the very least, can't express it in words. That's changing. I think. But we still have a large hunk of folks who would rather skip the nuts and bolts of doctrine and move on to something more exciting.

In fact, some of you have already tuned out on this chapter. Right? That only further indicates the great need to pass the torch of our faith from one generation to the next. To get young people to see the necessity of keeping pure the wonderful doctrines of truth. To not compromise those truths or let society pollute them. To not let secular humanism and situational ethics affect them.

"What are some of these doctrines?" you may be wondering. Good question. Let me just throw some of the "biggies" your way, although most of these have already come under attack in our rebellious society. Here is the Top Five countdown:

5. *Jesus is coming back* (Acts 1:10–11). We talked about that earlier. The apostles believed Jesus was coming back in their time. In every age Christians have awaited his coming. The Scriptures are full of promises about his second coming. Still, more people deny it today than at any other time.

4. *Only Jesus saves* (Acts 4:12). To me that's as plain as the nose on my face. But thousands of people add a half-dozen other requirements: baptism, communion, good works, the rosary, catechism, and church membership. Some even go so far as to say you must belong to a certain denomination (theirs, of course) to go to heaven. Hogwash!

3. *Man is sinful* (Rom 3:23). Society would have us believe man is basically good at heart. But man is a sinner at heart. That doesn't mean he's incapable of good; it just means he's incapable of pleasing God. Man can't pull himself up to heaven by his own bootstraps. No matter how culture changes, that never does.

2. *God's Word is inspired* (2 Tim. 3:16). This has sure caused a lot of stir in recent years. It has become more prevalent for new graduates to dismiss the Bible as "just another book." I was appalled to hear of a seminary professor in our city who recently drop-kicked the Bible across his classroom when he said, "This is what I think of the doctrine of inspiration." He blasphemed the faith. Now we're passing the torch to you. What will you do with it?

1. *God exists* (Heb. 11:6). Of course, this is the foundation for all doctrine. Only the fool says there is no God (Ps. 14:1). It would appear America has an abundant supply of fools these days.

Listen, it is not necessary for religious doctrine (teaching) to be as stale as the bread your school served you last semester. Doctrine is meaty, sure. But if it's dry, blame that on the cook, not on God. The challenge every Bible teacher and would-be Bible student ought to accept is this: keep your doctrine juicy, watch your life, and practice the truth you believe. Realize that behavior illustrates belief.

Just looking toward heaven when you crow isn't enough. If it were, then God would have made you a rooster!

The torch is passed,
Brent

14 Transition

Trading Places

And the things you have heard me say in the presence of many witnesses entrust to reliable men who will also be qualified to teach others (2 Tim. 2:2).

Dear Graduate,

You are moving from one point in your life to the next. You're in transition, which can be tough and strange—yet wonderful. You're trading places. Everything is now set in motion for you to become a part of the establishment. It will take a while, but soon, very soon, you will be one of us. And the course of the future for our country will be determined by you—all of you. All of *us*!

The other day I was thinking about my own transition from school days to adult ways. As much as I hate to admit it, I wasn't ready. But let me tell you something else: if somebody had merely suggested my immaturity to me at the time, I would have bitten his head off! Sure, I had all the answers, and the ones I didn't have I faked. Boy, was I about to get my "come-uppance" as Grandpa used to say.

That "come-uppance" refers to the hard knocks of transition. The knocks are harder for some than for others, but everybody gets them. If you want yours to be real hard, then be stubborn. How would *I* know? Listen, you're talking to an expert! My mind was, as someone once said, "like concrete—thoroughly mixed and permanently set."

"Be a nonconformist" was my motto in those days. I was not going to become like everybody else. Nothing wrong with that, and God likes individualism. He just doesn't like rebellion. Soon I learned that if there's anything a nonconformist hates, it's another nonconformist who doesn't conform to the prevailing standards of nonconformity. I also learned that stubbornness and nonconformity are a quick ticket to many of life's bumps and bruises. Guess who wised up!

I know now that this isn't the only transition you will face. There are others. Some are even harder than this one. But cheer up—at least there are some tip-offs to recognize a transition stage when it's coming. Mark these down:

Change Points. There are some natural points in life, like graduation, when you're going to go through a series of changes. Let me name the most outstanding ones to get ready for: finishing college, getting married, becoming a first-time parent (and the birth of *each* of your children), turning thirty, when school age comes for your first child, signing your first mortgage, beginning and settling into your career, the sale of your first home, the death of a parent, your first child's graduation, turning forty, your last child's graduation, your first child's marriage, the birth of your first grandchild, turning fifty (and each decade thereafter), and the death of your spouse. These are major transition experiences. And you thought graduation was a big deal!

Turning Points. Every now and then a particularly rough situation will come along—an intense trial that may mark a significant turning point in your life. When Saul of Tarsus was stricken by God on the Damascus Road, little did he know what a tremendous transformation he was about to experience. Saul would soon become Paul. The antagonist transformed into an apostle. When Moses sat down to supper in the desert one night, it never entered his mind what might happen. But in a flash God set a bush aflame with his

72

glorious presence, and Moses the Despondent became Moses the Deliverer. A turning point. You may face more than one or you may have only one in your entire lifetime. Several small turning points may work together to bring about one powerful transition. Or a single, supercharged circumstance may suddenly and drastically change you once and for all, forever. Maybe a sermon will be the big turning point for you, but there is an infinite list of other possibilities: a death, an accident, a new awareness, a lost love, a broken friendship, unemployment, a serious illness, a brush with death, a new responsibility, an unexpected blessing. All I know is that sometimes God brings us to a place where we feel we're hanging over the edge of a cliff and must do something—anything—to change our lives before it's tragically too late. That's a turning point.

Outposts. Moses needed an out-of-the-way burning bush before he was willing to make a change. David camped out in caves when he was fleeing from Saul or when his son Absalom overthrew the kingdom, and he wrote some of his best tunes there (see *Psalms for Graduates*). The Lord tutored Paul for three years on the backside of the desert before he was ready to accept the hardships he would suffer (Gal. 1:15–18). Elijah was fed by ravens at the brook called Cherith before God used him to deploy spiritual SDI (Strategic Defense Initiative) against the idol-worshipers on Mount Carmel. All these men had outpost experiences. Hard times of private learning. Days of deep inner struggle. Moments when they held on for dear life. Nobody else understood their burdens, so they carried the pressure alone. And God carried them through it. You may have an outpost experience someday. A time when you feel all alone—like you're wandering about with no purpose and need to battle to piece together who you are. Then there will be a quiet transition for you as you listen to the still, small voice of God guiding you. All the while, God is refining your maturity.

That sure beats being a nonconformist. Unless you're a glutton for "come-uppance."

Put away childish things,
Brent

15 **Productivity**
Top Gun

Our people must learn to devote themselves to doing what is good, in order that they may provide for daily necessities and not live unproductive lives (Titus 3:14).

Dear Graduate,

You may not have heard of William Wolcott, the great English artist who came to New York in 1924 to draw his impressions of the Big Apple. After spending a week to get a feel for the skyscraper city, he visited the office of an architect friend and colleague. Suddenly, the urge swept over him to sketch the city. He told his friend, "Please, I need some paper." His eyes darted like a cat's, and seeing some paper on the desk, he said, "May I use that?" The architect replied, "That's not sketching paper. That's just ordinary wrapping paper." The artist, afraid he would lose his inspiration, put his hand out for the paper and said, "Nothing is ordinary if you know how to use it." Wolcott made two sketches from the "ordinary wrapping paper." One later sold for a thousand dollars and the other for five hundred. Pretty productive. Wouldn't you say?

We all know we live in a success-oriented society. Millions want to climb the corporate ladder and eat pie in the sky. We're a people infatuated with success and all the status symbols that go with it: BMW's, big houses, a smart stock portfolio, an American Express card, and a new wardrobe from Giorgio of Beverly Hills. I was blown away recently when I listened to a large group of high school students talk about their goals and ambitions for life. They all wanted material things. Cars. Houses. Boats. Trips. Money. Not one spoke of wanting to serve God or even helping other people in some way.

No, I'm not trying to be super-spiritual. I'm all for being successful. God doesn't want you to flop, but he doesn't want you to flip out either. He desires that you have a fruitful life, touching the lives of many and bringing blessings to those who come your way. And God isn't down on material wealth as long as you don't crave it and live for it. If it comes, fine. If not, fine. God is still God, and you can be productive and fruitful, whatever your bank statement shows.

God is so interested in your success, so committed to you, that he laid out some simple rules of thumb for anyone desiring to be truly productive. Test them:

"Branch" Operations. Jesus taught his disciples this important piece of business sense: "'I am the vine; you are the branches. If a man remains in me and I in him, he will bear much fruit; apart from me you can do nothing'" (John 15:5). There you have the secret to becoming either a somebody or a nobody. If you do all you do for the Lord's sake and to please him, it counts forever. That's something! If you live only to please yourself and your selfish desires, you may have success—even great success—but only temporarily. That's really nothing! Be a branch, and remember who the Vine is. Branches cannot bear fruit on their own. They need the vine. Jesus is our Vine. Our lives must be tied up in him if we hope to be productive.

Soil Preparation. Bad soil always produces a bad crop. Plant among the rocks if you wish to harvest rocks. Don't cut back the thorns and thistles if you want to have them overrun your garden. But who wants that? So learn early that pearls were never meant for swine, just as a good idea was never meant for bad ground. Jesus taught, "'Still other seed fell on good soil, where it produced a crop—a hundred, sixty or thirty times what was sown'" (Matt.

13:8). Some people would call that being in the right place at the right time. Jesus called it good farming. Nothing brings a bumper crop like putting down the right seed, in the right place, at the right time. And nothing will make you productive like sharing your good ideas (and God's gospel!) with ready people, as God leads you.

Peculiar Germination. Any farmer knows that dry and apparently dead seeds bring life. When moistened under warm, rich soil, they germinate and burst into new growth. The death-to-life principle is not a new one. Jesus taught it as a staple of powerful productivity: "'I tell you the truth, unless a kernel of wheat falls to the ground and dies, it remains only a single seed. But if it dies it produces many seeds'" (John 12:24). If you do not fall to the ground, if you do not die to self, if you do not seal the coffin on your own desires, you cannot be truly fruitful. You must die—submit to God's design for you—fall to the ground, the *good* ground. Then you will rise up to be a branch. All you must do then is abide in the Vine and you will produce.

This is serious to you, I know. You're wondering what to do with your life. Sometimes you worry if you'll make it at all. You ask yourself, "Can I make it on my own? Will I be able to land a job decent enough to support a family?" You begin to feel plain and "just average," while everybody else around you appears to have superior intelligence, poise, and talent. You run a quick comparison and think you lose. But your youth bounces back, and you can hold out hope through your grimness, if you recall the lessons of Jesus at these times. Then, when your ordinariness is ever-present in your thoughts, listen to Willy Wolcott: "Nothing is ordinary if you know how to use it."

God knows how—and he will show you!

Bloom where you're planted,
Brent

The Magna Charta of Faith

Hebrews

*Standing somewhere in the assembled crowd is a Jew,
born of the tribe of Levi and of the house of Aaron, thus
by every right a priest. But he has become a Christian, so
this splendid Temple with its gorgeous ritual, sanctified by
Holy Writ and by traditions reaching back century after
century in time, is no longer for him. . . . He goes from
scroll to scroll, finding in all his Scriptures unexplained
ceremonies, unsatisfied longings, unfulfilled prophecies.
Deciding to stake his all on the despised and rejected Jesus
of Nazareth, he becomes a Christian, makes his faith
known, and is cut off from his people. His outraged
parents disinherit him, cast him out of the family and
outside the camp, hold a funeral for him, and consider
him dead. His heart aches for his loved ones, for the close-
knit family ties of the Jews. Missing the cheer and comfort
of home, missing the rich ritual in which he has been
reared, missing the synagogue and its forms, he begins to
wonder if he should go back. The epistle to the Hebrews
was written for him.*

John Phillips

The Magna Charta of Faith

Hebrews

*Standing somewhere in the assembled crowd is a Jew,
born of the tribe of Levi and of the house of Aaron, thus
by every right a priest. But he has become a Christian, so
this splendid Temple with its gorgeous ritual, sanctified by
Holy Writ and by traditions reaching back century after
century in time, is no longer for him. . . . He goes from
scroll to scroll, finding in all his Scriptures unexplained
ceremonies, unsatisfied longings, unfulfilled prophecies.
Deciding to stake his all on the despised and rejected Jesus
of Nazareth, he becomes a Christian, makes his faith
known, and is cut off from his people. His outraged
parents disinherit him, cast him out of the family and
outside the camp, hold a funeral for him, and consider
him dead. His heart aches for his loved ones, for the close-
knit family ties of the Jews. Missing the cheer and comfort
of home, missing the rich ritual in which he has been
reared, missing the synagogue and its forms, he begins to
wonder if he should go back. The epistle to the Hebrews
was written for him.*

John Phillips

16 Hardness

Defensive Holding

As it has just been said: "Today, if you hear his voice, do not harden your hearts as you did in the rebellion" (Heb. 3:15).

Dear Graduate,

Shhh! Don't let this word get out, but a part of me—probably a crazy part—is a secret New York Yankees baseball fan. While I believe that the day George Steinbrenner gives up ownership of the team will be the greatest day in Yankee history, I like the team in spite of him. There's just something about all that tradition that attracts a true fan. Think of all the greats who have suited up for the Bronx Bombers: Babe Ruth, Lou Gehrig, Joe Dimaggio, Yogi Berra, Mickey Mantle, Whitey Ford, and Reggie Jackson. And, of course, don't forget the pinstripes.

A few years ago, at a meeting of the Fellowship of Christian Athletes, one of my all-time favorite Yankees, former second baseman Bobby Richardson, offered a prayer that is a classic in brevity and poignancy: "Dear God. Your will, nothing more, nothing less, nothing else. Amen."

The shocking truth of the matter is, it is possible—yes, an ever-present danger—that a born-again Christian can become hardened to the God who loves him. When sinners spurn God, that does not much surprise us. But when a forgiven believer does, it sends chills to our bones.

What was the Hebrews writer referring to when he spoke of "the rebellion"? Well, that was a day of terrible disobedience and refers to the children of Israel. God had brought them out of Egypt, fed them with manna, quenched their thirst with water from the rock, and even guided them with the cloud of his presence. And yet, they still had a bit of old Egypt in them. God was ready to give them the grand prize, better than any lottery pay-off, but they were afraid to take it. God's will was for them to march into Canaan and inherit the land. But the chosen people didn't listen to God. They didn't listen to his two wise spies either. They ignored Joshua and Caleb and agreed with the ten other spies, who warned the people that it was very scary over in Canaan. That provoked God! From where the people were camped, they could have cruised into the Promised Land in a week and a half. But because of their rebellion and hard hearts, God sent them back into the wilderness. All totalled, they went around in circles for forty years! All because of one day of rebellion. All because of hardness to God's will.

This straight-from-the-hip letter to the Hebrews alludes to that day of rebellion and is a warning to contemporary Christians. God wants to lead us, too. And if we become calloused to his gentle guidance, we are in danger of living a "wilderness" life.

There's a little of the old Egypt in all of us. If we listen to it, then silently and subtly we will grow cold to God's will. We may not recognize the almost undetectable changes at first, but our family and friends will. The symptoms of hardness are obvious. That is, unless it's happening to you.

An Insensitive Spirit. New Christians are so sensitive to the Holy Spirit. He has only to speak softly, and they are immediately convicted of some sin or habit that needs janitorial service. Babes in Christ are hungry to grow and long to understand more of God's Word. They are eager to tell everybody about how God has forgiven them. For them, attending church is a pleasure instead of a ritual.

Life is full, and their eyes are wide-open to its joys. That sort of balances out once a believer is discipled for a while. But whenever a Christian becomes insensitive to God's Spirit, that's a sure sign of a hardening of his spiritual arteries. He's on the road to a spiritual heart attack! If the last thing you want is to be thick-skinned toward God, then don't let yourself tune out the tender talk of his Spirit.

A Numb Conscience. Several times, Paul wrote to young Timothy to exhort him to protect his conscience. If God's warning buzzer is not working, you have no alarm system to alert you whenever Satan gets into your life. First Timothy 4:2 goes so far as to say that there are some "whose consciences have been seared as with a hot iron." Nothing numbs the skin like a bad burn. And nothing reveals flint-heartedness like a conscience with third-degree burns.

A Dissatisfied Disposition. Paul sent a pungent note to the Galatians (as we noticed earlier) and reminded them that a spirit-filled Christian is joyful. He told the Philippians that the natural mood of a believer is contentment. And he taught the Thessalonians to give thanks in every thing. When one of God's kids turns into a snarling, critical Jonah, the water spigot to the free flow of God's Spirit has been shut off. It is not uncommon for apathy and dullness to hang their hats in the heart of such a brutish soul. It soon becomes clear that he has gulped down a powerful anesthetic and is now as spiritually dead as Ananias and Sapphira (see Acts 5:1–10).

But thank God for the words of another Yankee, Yogi Berra: "It's never over till it's over." And it's not too late for those who have become unyielding as rocks to let the plow of God do its work. Even if it seems late in the game, you can still change your line-up card and put God's will at the top. Nothing more. Nothing less. Nothing else. Right, Bobby?

Listen to the Coach,
Brent

17 Maturity

The Peter Pan *Syndrome*

*Therefore let us leave the elementary teachings about Christ
and go on to maturity . . .* (Heb. 6:1).

Dear Graduate,

Remember Wendy, Michael, and John? And Never-Never Land?
And Tinkerbell? And the Lost Boys? And Captain Hook? They are all
part of that gigantic classic, *Peter Pan*. Of course, you know it is a
story about the sad and wonderful occasion of growing up. Wendy is
spending her last night in the family nursery when Peter Pan comes
to find his shadow. Then he takes Wendy, Michael, and John with
him to Never-Never Land, where children are children forever.

Glance back at the key verse. It looks as if the Hebrews writer
knew some believers who were playing spiritual Peter Pan. They
didn't want to grow up into mature disciples. They liked being
babied. Maybe most of all they liked being free from responsibility.
Listen to the bullets Mr. Hebrews fired from point-blank range in his
masterful letter:

> In fact, though by this time you ought to be teachers, you need
> someone to teach you the elementary truths of God's word all over
> again. You need milk, not solid food! Anyone who lives on milk,
> being still an infant, is not acquainted with the teaching about
> righteousness. But solid food is for the mature, who by constant use

have trained themselves to distinguish good from evil [Heb. 5:12–14].

Have you noticed that this is still a problem among Christians today? In too many cases we have a lot of slush and very little substance. I know. I've seen some of it myself. There are too many disciples who talk of Jesus but do not walk with him. Their faith may be enough to save them from hell, but it does not cure them of their anger or bitterness or vengeance or gossip. Does such a faith really save anybody? I wonder.

Still, I am sure there are many Jesus people who mean well; just as a child cannot help his immaturity, they seem unable to help theirs. Except for one important consideration: they have chosen to stay small. Little people have little requirements, even though they have big problems. Keeping requirements to a minimum is attractive to some folks. So don't feel too sorry for anybody who is out to lunch in Never-Never Land when he is long overdue in climbing out of his spiritual crib.

Don't get me wrong. None of us is a full-grown adult in Christ all of the time. I don't know if we should be. Actually, we waver back and forth from one state to another. Notice I said "state," not "stage." A "stage" is a temporary phase we pass through. It lasts for a while and then it's over. A "state" is a condition, a frame of mind. As God's kids, I think we experience at least four "states." Sometimes all in one day!

Infancy/Childhood. This is a fascinating time. For babes in Christ, everything about God is so new, so refreshing, so alive. A magical glow falls over a newborn Christian. It is a precious period in grace-style growing. But, as we have seen, spiritual childhood isn't supposed to last forever. Just as in secular life we are soon fed up with a twenty-two-year-old who acts like a four-year-old, so do Christians quickly get their fill of a fellow-believer who needs to get with the program and live some of what he learned eons ago. Because we're all selfish at heart, we're prone to drift into this state of childish egotism from time to time. When you don't get your way, it's up to *you* to decide to stop sucking your thumb.

Adolescence. Spiritual teenagers? Yeah, I think we all experience this state now and then. The first time you reach this level of maturity it feels weird. As your yearnings for liberty set in, stirrings of independence may cause you to question your beliefs. It can be a dangerous time in Christian growth. Some believers throw off all their good sense in this state. Usually it is a healthy time, though. After a year or so of growing in Christ, it is normal for disciples to go beyond some of the childish ideas they had about Christianity in their early months as believers. Then it is time to become more mature. Again, however, we sometimes drift back into this mood of "testing the things of God." It is not unlikely for us to act as if we've just finished supper at our Lord's Table and now say, "Jesus, can I have the keys tonight?" We want to do all our own driving, instead of leaving the wheel in his hands when the road surface or weather is rough.

Adulthood. You figured this was next, I'm sure. After a few years of following Christ, it is quite normal—even reasonable—for a believer to reach a certain acceptable level of maturity. An "adult" disciple knows how to apply truth to daily living. He faces temptation with courage. Victory belongs to the believer at this point on the growth chart. One of the unfortunate side effects is an occasional case of super-sainthood. Just as parents are sometimes perturbed with their children, so spiritual adults are sometimes impatient and judgmental toward youngsters in Christ.

Old Age. You don't have to be advanced in years to experience wisdom, to wear the crown of maturity. Seeing situations as Jesus does—and responding to them as he would—this is the peak of our spiritual growth. Most of us go only for short visits to this summit before we slip back into our childhood egotism, or teenage rebelliousness, or adult complacency. Also, being old in years doesn't mean you will automatically be a wise and noble spiritual giant. Some of the biggest babies I've ever known in the family of God were senior citizens. (That's my "adult" state talking.) Just the same, there is no pleasure quite like the ripeness of spiritual wisdom.

It may take many years to scale the mountain of Christian maturity. Some never do. They're busy talking about Captain Hook. That's too bad. Wendy finally came home and left the nursery. And even Peter Pan found his shadow.

Here's hoping you'll find yours,
Brent

18 Legacy

Uncommon Valor

All these people were still living by faith when they died. They did not receive the things promised; they only saw them and welcomed them from a distance. And they admitted that they were aliens and strangers on earth (Heb. 11:13).

Dear Graduate,

The other day I read an anecdote about a fellow who had dropped off a cliff and was plummeting toward the rocks below when he luckily grabbed the small twig of a tree that was growing out of a crack in the side of the perilous precipice. (I wouldn't put a whole lot of stock in this being a *true* story if I were you!) Hanging there, what seemed like a mile from the jagged rocks and rushing rapids below, he tried not to look down. Terrified, he cried out to the sky, "Help! Is anybody up there?"

Out of the clouds came the words, "I am here."

"Who are you?" he called back.

"I am your God," the voice replied.

"Can you help me?" The man tried not to sound too desperate.

"Have faith," the thunderous voice commanded. "Let go."

The man frowned and looked down at the ominous view beneath him. Then he looked back toward the clouds and shouted, "Is anybody else up there?"

I don't know about you, but I can relate to that story. There have been times in my life when I felt like I was dangling from a lone tree branch on the side of some cliff. In fear I cried out for God to deliver me from my trial, and he said, "Let go, my son, and I will catch you. Rest in my arms, and I will carry you." Inside I was thinking, *Yes, Lord, but it's a long way down. What if you accidentally miss me?* O me of little faith!

How could I write to you about Hebrews and leave out at least an honorable mention of the Faith Hall of Fame in Hebrews, chapter eleven? This is such a fantastic passage of Scripture that whole books have been written on it. You're in luck. I'm only going to write one letter, and I'm only going to press across one point: *leave a legacy*. I might say that more than once before I sign off, but that's just to drive home the point. My repetition is not merely for the sake of being cute. If you leave a legacy, you will do something few Christians do. And even fewer Americans.

What is a legacy? It is a gift received from an ancestor. Originally, "legacy" referred to great wealth left to some lucky duck in a will. That's not the legacy I want you to leave. Leave a spiritual legacy of uncommon valor. Pass down a great heritage of faith. Be a standout for God and bequeath that to your children and theirs. Be somebody for the cause of Christ. Weather great storms. Endure hard battles. Capture the enemies' flag. Hand down the dignity of discipleship. *Leave a legacy.*

Start building now. A legacy never grows overnight. Spiritual wealth takes years to accumulate. Do you think you can merely sit upon your rocking chair tomorrow and make wide the eyes of children with your stories of the lions in Daniel's den and David's mighty men? No, it doesn't work that way. Instead, tomorrow you will sit in the den yourself and find out whether or not God still has the power to shut the mouths of wild beasts. Those lions are financial woes, heartaches and heartbreaks, a tough row to hoe in college, a marriage that requires more work than you expected, a career that is shaky. Tomorrow you will also find your own smooth stones and discover if God is still in the giant-killing business. And the giant may be depression, a crippling disease, the birth of a mentally retarded child, or the sudden death of your mate. No, you are not ready for rocking-chair wisdom. That is for grandpas and grandmas. And maybe you will be one someday. If you are, how can you *leave a legacy* unless you spend these next years building it? Do not wait until you are thirty or forty to start. You may not live that long, and then you will have no legacy to leave.

Read our lead-in verse. The first sentence says it all: "All these people were still living by faith when they died" (Heb. 11:13). What a testimony! Wouldn't that be a great epitaph for a tombstone? *He was still living by faith when he died.* That's a real legacy. Those Old Testament ancients left a legacy. And the whole Jewish nation is justifiably proud of that legacy until this day. Their ancestors died with their boots on.

Build right. If all you leave behind is a pile of material possessions and a fat bankroll, so what? Will that matter when the graves are opened and the Book of Life is laid out before the throne of God? (Yeah, I know I'm being sort of preachy. I probably sound like your mother, but this is important stuff.) Accumulate blessings instead. There is no wealth as precious as answers to prayer in seasons when you trusted God. Listen, someday *you* are going to be the mom or dad. How will you help your kids—like you need help now—if you have not been working on your legacy? It will be a sad day if you cannot hand down a powerful faith that looks up to God. Whether or not you understand it fully, you must begin building right habits of devotion and a life of integrity now, or you won't have it later. You need it now in a great way. But, believe me, you'll need it even more later. If you don't start right now, it will be even harder to do it later.

The time has come for you to consider the bigger picture. You must begin to think less of yourself and prepare a way for the next generation. I'll probably see you on the side of the cliff, hanging on to a twig for dear life. It is the place where lions go hungry and giants fall with a thud—because it is the place where legacies are made.

Keep your boots on,
Brent

Proverbs Digest

James

The Epistle leaves on us the impression that it comes from a vigorous personality, a strong, immoveable personality, a real pillar of the church, as James was declared by Paul to be. . . . The author plunges at once into his subject with a bold paradox, and his short, decisive sentences fall like hammer strokes. His rebukes contain some of the sharpest invective in the New Testament, and he knows when irony will serve him best.

Alexander Ross

19 Favoritism

And Justice for All

But if you show favoritism, you sin and are convicted by the law as lawbreakers (James 2:9).

Dear Graduate,

Favoritism is a lot like prejudice. It means that for one reason or another you choose some people over others. Maybe you've heard about John Howard Griffin. He's the guy who was courageous enough to change the color of his skin from white to black—in 1959, which was not exactly a pleasant time in American history for negroes. Griffin believed he would never understand the plight of blacks unless he could somehow become one. So he darkened his skin by using oral medication, sunlamp treatments, and stains. Then he traveled through the South.

The results were heartbreaking. Griffin received treatment that was almost inhuman. He was disallowed from riding certain vehicles or sitting where he wanted. Certain restaurants refused to serve him food. There were hotels that denied him a room. Certain rest rooms were off limits to him, as were some public drinking fountains. When he wasn't being persecuted or ridiculed, he was being slighted and cheated. Griffin was so shocked and stirred by what he learned that he put his experiences down on paper in his now-famous book, *Black Like Me*.

But favoritism is more than intolerance toward a particular racial or ethnic group. Choosing the rich over the poor, that's favoritism. So is catering to the pretty over the plain. Or the tall over the short. The blonde over the brunette. The intelligent over the simple. The pleasant over the outrageous. Clean-shaven men over those with beards. Ladies who apply their makeup correctly (by *your* standards) over those who cake it on. People who wear fashionable suits and dresses to church over those who wear blue jeans. Those who sing old hymns of the faith over those who prefer Amy Grant's latest hit.

Even thinking more highly of one person as compared to another can be a form of favoritism. Stay with me on this—I haven't gone mad! Naturally you love some people more than others. If you didn't, *you* would be the kook. You'd be a little off balance upstairs if you didn't love your mother with a much deeper affection than any ordinary person you met on the street. And no one would label you a "respecter of persons" if you pulled for your brother or sister to win in a race or a game. Not even God. In fact, we probably would wonder about you if you didn't.

Of course, there are also things that attract us to certain people as our friends. Like the way our personalities hit it off, the common interests we share, living in the same neighborhood, and being near the same age. These are the normal things that nurture relationships, but that's not what I'm talking about. When a Christian just looks at another person and begins to form opinions, that is foolish. And that's what I'm talking about, since we all tend to do this. To a certain extent we can't help it. At least not without a strict retraining of our thinking. Stereotyping seems to be part of the American Way.

Think "poor." What image comes to mind? Some unkempt man or woman with barely enough food to live and hardly enough clothes to stay warm? *Bless their hearts,* you may think, *they make little contribution to our society. They are too uneducated to do much good.* Really? Jesus would find that generalization interesting. He was always a few dollars short for his next meal, but we could hardly

94

say he had nothing to contribute. Some of the people who have left the greatest mark on history arose from poverty. The next time you see a poor person, you may be seeing a parent of tomorrow's next president. If you see nothing else, see Jesus.

Think "rich." What image comes to mind? Affluent, powerful, intelligent, and responsible? Probably close enough. But do you also see someone who is better off, more capable, a cut above the rest? If you do, your stereotyping is showing through. Be careful. Human beings cannot be added up like a column of figures. A book I once read about the ministry of deacons suggested that bank presidents make the best chairmen. It's a good thing the apostles didn't think that way. Imagine what an overwhelming difference it would have made in the early church if the president of the First National Commercial Bank of Jerusalem had headed the board of deacons. Why, just think of the results if Jesus had taken a lesson from this narrow-minded advice when selecting his disciples. Could stockbrokers and merchants have done a better job of being the first disciples than those lowly fishermen? (Now are you starting to understand where James was coming from?)

Here's some things about Christian love and how it relates to showing favoritism:

Love doesn't mean "like." You may not *like* a person, but you can still love him—or rather you can let God love him through you. His (or her) habits may aggravate you, and you may not desire this person to be your intimate friend. And yet, you can decide within your will to love that person anyway. No, it may not be an emotional, affectionate love, but it will be love just the same. This will help to keep you from putting at a disadvantage those you might naturally dislike at first. It will teach you to give all people a fair shake.

It meets people where they are. Love builds people up; it doesn't tear them down. Love goes out to meet people; it doesn't expect them to improve themselves first. Love helps people to start getting better by encouraging them where they are; it even pitches in to help them. Christian love does not set demands upon people that they must satisfy before they can measure up. It shows no such favoritism. Christian love is color-blind, and money-blind, and gender-blind. It is careful to presuppose nothing.

Christian love despises stereotypes, and it longs to break the mold. Like John Howard Griffin did.

Favor not by appearances,
Brent

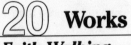 **Works**

Faith-Walking

In the same way, faith by itself, if it is not accompanied by action, is dead (James 2:17).

Dear Graduate,

If you don't have a copy of Chuck Swindoll's book, *The Quest for Character,* I recommend you get one. Borrow if you have to. I particularly like the quotation he includes from Robert Pirsig's peculiarly titled book, *Zen and the Art of Motorcycle Maintenance.* Pirsig's statements about "gumption" really tickled my heart. More Christians need to hear it.

> I like the word "gumption" because it's so homely and so forlorn and so out of style it looks as if it needs a friend and it isn't likely to reject anyone who comes along. . . . A person filled with gumption doesn't sit around dissipating and stewing about things. He's at the front of the train of his own awareness, watching to see what's up the track and meeting it when it comes. . . . If you're going to repair a motorcycle, an adequate supply of gumption is the first and most important tool. If you haven't got that you might as well gather up all the other tools and put them away, because they won't do you any good. . . . Therefore the thing that must be monitored at all times and preserved before anything else is gumption.

Gumption is what many Christians want but do not have. That's what is so much needed in young disciples today but seems to be in short supply.

James really got carried away by this subject. Work! Work! Work! He wanted Christians to work. In fact, he so much believed that Christians should be people of action that he gives the impression in his letter that anybody who claims to have faith in Jesus but doesn't serve him is just fooling himself. He's no more saved than the man in the moon (whoever that may be).

Well, what do you think? Do we have to do good works in order to be saved? No! No! No! A million times, NO! We are saved by grace through faith, and not by works. Remember letter eight? However, a faith that doesn't work is dead. As the famous theologian John Calvin said, "It is faith alone that justifies, but faith that justifies can never be alone." Or, as another put it, "Faith is not believing in spite of evidence, but obeying in spite of consequence." Real faith reveals itself in obedience. And obedience reveals itself in good works. Therefore, genuine faith and Christian works are inseparable partners.

Back to the problem that disciples today are short on gumption. Without gumption it is impossible to get any real job done. And not only is our job big, but there aren't many workers. Consider the desperate situation in the church of the poor fellow who penned this letter:

Dear Friend:

Our church membership	1400
Nonresident membership	75
Balance left to do the work	1325
Elderly who have already done their part	25
Balance left to do the work	1300
Sick and shut-in folks	25
Balance left to do the work	1275
Membership who did not pledge	350
Christmas and Easter members	300
Tired and overworked members	300

Balance left to do the work	325
Alibiers	200
Members who are busy elsewhere	123
Balance left to do the work	2

That's just you and me—and brother, you'd better get busy because it's too much for me!

WANTED: LABORERS FOR CHRIST'S HARVEST. That, in short, is what I'm getting at. We need your help. Whether it's in the local church, on the mission field, at a community rescue mission, with nursing homes, for orphans, to reach teenagers, at a counseling center, or just in your neighborhood, we need your help. Who will help the poor if we do not? Who will give water to the thirsty? Who will clothe the naked? Who will carry the gospel?

A true Christian practices the truth. His faith is dynamic—it springs into action. Real Christians care enough to do something. They are not much into Zen, and motorcycle maintenance is, at the most, only a hobby to them. But they've got a handle on the most important tool for any job: gumption.

Tri-"umph,"
Brent

21 **Worldliness**

All That Glitters

You adulterous people, don't you know that friendship with the world is hatred toward God? Anyone who chooses to be a friend of the world becomes an enemy of God (James 4:4).

Dear Graduate,

According to ancient mythology—and I promise you that I'm not much on mythology—when Hercules fought with Antaeus, every time he threw his opponent to the ground, he jumped up again stronger than ever. Antaeus gained his strength by coming into contact with the earth. Hercules conquered him at last only by holding him in the air away from the source of his power. Finally, Antaeus grew weaker and weaker until, totally exhausted, he was no match for Hercules.

Mythology or not, that scenario is brimming with spiritual application. Although the believer has Herculean power in the Holy Spirit, he also has an Antaeus fighting for attention within him. And that Antaeus wars with the Spirit for control of the disciple. The spirit of Antaeus loves the world, drawing power from contact with the things of this earth. So the more a Christian pals around with worldliness, the stronger Antaeus becomes within him. The deeper his roots grow in this cosmos, this temporary system, the quicker Antaeus arises to combat Hercules. But whenever a Christian grabs hold of his passions, ambitions, and hunger for the things of this world and tears them away from the source of their strength, get ready for the Hercules Show. That's when it's winning time for the Holy Spirit. The longer a believer lives a life separated from worldliness, the mightier in spirit he becomes.

As someone has said, "If it's really true that all the world is a stage, then God's children should have stage fright." We must pry ourselves away from the magnetic pull of the world. Remember, we're pilgrims. Not that we can't enjoy the bounties of earth. We can. But loving them, craving them—that's another story. Maybe you should stick a spiritual thermometer under your tongue and see if you have a fever for the flavor of the world:

Which disturbs you most?
A lost soul in hell . . . or a scratch on your new car?
Missing a worship service . . . or missing a day's work?
A sermon ten minutes too long . . . or lunch a half-hour late?
Your church not growing . . . or your garden not growing?
Your Bible unopened . . . or your newspaper not read?
The church work being neglected . . . or your homework neglected?
Missing a good Bible study . . . or missing your favorite T.V. show?
The millions who don't know Christ . . . or your inability to keep up with the neighbors?
The cry of multitudes for bread . . . or your desire for another piece of German chocolate cake?
Your tithing decreasing . . . or your income decreasing?
Which really disturbs you most?

James was death on worldliness. By the way, what did James mean by "the world," and what is "worldliness"? The world is our society apart from God. It is the things of man: money, materialism, and humanist philosophy, for starters. Worldliness is having an attachment to those things, letting them drive deep tent stakes within you instead of keeping the heart of a pilgrim who sees himself as only a wanderer in this world. It is becoming too familiar and comfortable in these surroundings, like Lot did in Sodom.

Back to James. He named the world as the "enemy of God." Now get this clear: James didn't say that God is the world's enemy. God loves the world. James said that the world is God's enemy. In other words, this earthly system is Satan's way of fighting back. Worldliness is his weapon against mankind, and he uses it to capture us because he knows that man is dear to the heart of God.

What does this mean? Simply this: if we sign a treaty with the world and become its allies, we have made ourselves enemies of God. The worldly system will never please him. It is corrupt, degenerate, and unholy. God hates the system and will one day judge all those who have loved it.

Declaring war against God is pretty risky business. But that doesn't stop some so-called Christians. In the same way a person enters an adulterous physical relationship, one can commit spiritual adultery by becoming intertwined with the world. Soon, what started as "innocent" friendship explodes into total infatuation. The trap is shut!

Then what happens? Antaeus jumps up to battle with the Holy Spirit. Whether or not the Herculean power can conquer Antaeus depends upon how affectionately that giant is nestling in the arms of the voluptuous world. How far has "Mother Earth" enticed Antaeus? If she has won his heart, Antaeus has the victory and has defeated one more Christian. That, my friend, is no myth!

Grow shallow roots in the earth,
Brent

Bulk Mail

1 and 2 Peter

The differences [between the two epistles] arise mainly out of the subjects treated in the two, and the design which the writer seems to have kept constantly in view. In the first, he sought to comfort, strengthen, and sustain his persecuted brethren; this is his supreme aim. In the second he is anxious to warn and to shield those whom he addresses as to impending dangers more disastrous and more to be feared than the sufferings inflicted by a hostile world.

William Moorehead

# 22 Hospitality

Angels Unawares

Offer hospitality to one another without grumbling
(1 Peter 4:9).

Dear Graduate,

You know from studying history and geography that East Berlin is Communist-controlled, and West Berlin is free. The story is told of some people in East Berlin who one day took a truckload of garbage and dumped it on the West Berlin side. A questionable gesture of neighborliness, I'm sure you'd agree.

It would have been in most people's minds to return the favor in kind, and maybe the West Berliners were tempted for a moment. But instead they took a truckload of canned goods, bread, and milk. They stacked it neatly on the East Berlin side and put a sign on the top. The placard read: EACH GIVES WHAT HE HAS.

Though somewhat sarcastic in this example, that is the core of hospitality. Sharing whatever you have (the good things, that is). Hospitable people are warm, kind, and generous. They have open hearts and open houses and offer a standing invitation for a visit. These folks aren't just acting out a showy put-on either. No, they have simply learned the orders of Christian basic training: "Share with God's people who are in need. Practice hospitality" (Rom. 12:13).

I have had Christians tell me: "Hey! I don't want a bunch of people over at my house. I don't even want friends hanging around me. Just let me go back and forth from church. Learning the Bible is all I'm interested in. Leave me out of the social stuff." That would be fine except for one little snag. If a person is going to "learn the Bible," he is obligating himself to obey it. God's Word isn't just for entertainment or even for knowledge. And the Bible is plain-spoken on the hospitality issue. Jesus makes no provision for unfriendly, selfish believers.

Take good old Publius, for example. Once when Paul was traveling through Malta, he came to the estate of the chief island official. (You guessed it, his name was Publius.) Acts 28:7 says this Publius welcomed Paul and his buddies into his home and entertained them hospitably for three days. You can imagine how much damage that troop of guys did to the icebox in three days. But Publius didn't mind. He was glad to have Paul and the gang in for fellowship.

You know, though, entertaining house guests isn't the only way of showing hospitality. (By the way, have you noticed the root word of hospitality is "hospital?" A place of healing.) There are no limits to creative kindness. Why even the story of the Good Samaritan is really about hospitality.

Last year our family was traveling home from a wonderful ski trip in the Colorado Rockies. It was dark and we had been on the road for several hours. In fact, we had switched to a lesser-used highway because the main interstate had been closed because of drifting snow. We planned to cross back over when it was reopened. Much to our delight, the radio newscaster finally told us all roads were open, just about the time we were leaving Colorado. We were so excited to find a clear side road that we didn't notice how the strong winds had been filling the ditches with snow.

Suddenly we came over a hill into a massive snow drift that was covering the entire road. There was no time to stop. We were in it. Really in it! Up to the doors! Stuck! And the temperature was thirty degrees below zero, counting the wind-chill factor. I couldn't budge the car, and the drift blanketed the whole road for at least two hundred yards. It was a nightmare.

After a few minutes of waiting, I felt a sense of panic creeping over me. Jane was trying to remain calm, but with two young children asking questions from the back seat, it was hard for her not to worry. With no cars in sight, I began attempting anything that might help free our snowbound station wagon. When I was about frozen, two headlights appeared in the distance behind me. *At last some help has arrived,* I thought. But the car turned back. I guessed that they had not seen us. My prayer life was becoming fervent—maybe more fervent than at any other time in my life. I was almost reduced to trying to make a deal with God when another vehicle approached us. This time it brought help in the form of two young men.

For an hour we dug and pushed. The wagon rocked and rolled upon its bed of snow like the Beach Boys at an all-night concert. Finally, with one exhaustive push, the recently transformed snowmobile was free. I began thanking the young men who had been so hospitable as to stop. They were college students. Wouldn't you know it—they attended a Christian college! And they really knew the meaning of Good Samaritan hospitality.

Later, when we were back on the main interstate, Jane asked, "Honey, do you suppose those two guys were actually angels?" That really perked up the kids. They were fascinated at the possibility that we had entertained "angels unawares," as Hebrews 13:2 (KJV) mentions. I told them that playing in snow was strange entertainment for angels. "But who knows," I said, hoping to further pique their curiosity, "maybe they *were* angels. One thing's for sure—if they were angels, they won't have any need for that fifty-dollar check I wrote them."

It was a long three weeks, waiting for our monthly bank statement. And I suppose we were all a bit disappointed when we saw the check had been cashed. But then, maybe they really were angels and only cashed the check to keep their identity a secret from us. It's fun to believe that, anyway.

The way I figure it, I owe a debt to any poor, wandering stranger. Whether he eats at my table or needs a tow from the snow, I've got a debt to pay. Hospitality requires my generosity. Much was given to me, now much is required.

Somewhere in West Berlin some wise folks still laugh at the lesson they taught the East Berliners—one of kindness and hospitality. And maybe—just maybe—there are two angels chuckling beside the throne of Jesus about the night they played in the snow with me. The night they made Publius proud.

Catch the drift?
Brent

23 Exploitation

Ruthless People

In their greed these teachers will exploit you with stories they have made up. Their condemnation has long been hanging over them, and their destruction has not been sleeping (2 Peter 2:3).

Dear Graduate,

The words of Thomas Merton on the subject of love in *No Man Is an Island* absolutely grab me every time I read them: "Love seeks one thing only: the good of the one loved. It leaves all other secondary effects to take care of themselves. Love, therefore, is its own reward." What an intense thought! If there ever was a day in which that brand of love was so needed, it is this one. The 1990s promise to give new meaning to dog-eat-dog behavior.

Unfortunately, religion is at the center of much of our society's exploitation, and that is likely to continue. Bulletin: It's been that way for centuries. The sex and money scandals of the late 1980s will long be remembered because of the shock and distrust they caused. But they weren't the first nor the last rip-offs or disappointments served up by so-called Christians. Things like this date back to the days of the apostles.

That's right. Just read Peter's words at the top of this letter. In his lifetime there actually were religious leaders who had it in their minds to con people out of their money or whatever else they could get. They were slick and smooth. Cool operators. All in the name of God and righteousness. So it shouldn't surprise us when we see hucksters playing the odds in a similar style today.

Why am I writing you about this? For the same reason Peter did: to warn you to be alert. Don't let yourself get sucked in by these types of people or groups. They can be ruthless, even while wearing a gentle, endearing smile.

You probably already know that this world of ours is not always a wonderland. Not only is it tough to live down here, it's not even a great place for tourists. While our world has its moments of splendor, some parts and some of its people can be a horrible place to visit. My point is: be prepared. Be on guard. Otherwise you may fall victim to the devil's con job. There's nothing he'd love more than to sting you with the tricks of a weird religious group. With that he could discredit Christianity in your eyes and in the minds of those who see you tumble.

Before I continue with the tactics of ruthless people, let me set something straight: not all Christians are on the take. Not every preacher wants to build an empire and become famous. There are still countless people who believe in sacrifice rather than success. Don't lose heart. Be sure there will be con artists in your generation, but there will be honest people too. Good people. Trustworthy people.

Not like Jacob (you know, he of Jacob-and-Esau fame in Gen. 27). Remember how he pretended to be Esau by dressing in his brother's clothes, wrapping his arms in skins so he, too, would be "hairy"—all so his blind father wouldn't recognize him?

That's an "exploiter" for you. Taking advantage of someone in order to seize personal gain.

But if Jake fooled his father, he had already exploited Esau—like the day he conned him out of his blessing (Gen. 25:29–34). A little study of Jacob's methods reveal to us exactly how ruthless people operate. They take advantage of three basic things:

A Moment of Vulnerability. Esau was hungry, so Jake offered to trade him food for the blessing. Esau was vulnerable. It was a moment of weakness for him. How sneaky of his brother! That's why people who have been hurt work real hard at not being vulnerable. They don't want to be "taken" again. And yet, if we do not allow ourselves to be vulnerable within the bounds of godly wisdom, it will be hard for us to show love. We'll be wrapped in our paranoia and insecurity, trying to prevent ourselves from being cheated. It is more important for us to remain open, if even to be fooled a second time, than to clam up and harden ourselves to those who dare to show us love.

A Lack of Insight. Part of the con was Esau's fault. He wasn't enough on the ball to know how precious his father's blessing was to him. What he did would be the equivalent of your swapping a place in your parents' will with the owner of the local McDonald's—in exchange for a Big Mac. If we are to avoid being exploited, we will need spiritual insight. God promises wisdom to those who ask him. Those who don't know him are sitting ducks. How about you?: Do you have the power of understanding and the gift of discernment?

The Tendency to Be Gullible. Poor Esau. He was so naive he didn't really know what hit him. Not until afterwards. Then it was too late. Some people are like that. A salesman always has the perfect lemon for them. They seem to stumble repeatedly into bad relationships. Romance always deals them a busted hand. They just about fall for anything. That's Esau! And the ruthless know an Esau when they see him, so the short con has already begun.

Yes, Thomas Merton was right. *Love is its own reward.* But what he didn't say was: *Exploitation is its own destruction.* What goes around comes around. Jacob got his. All the ruthless get theirs eventually. For no man is an island.

Always watch the dealer,
Brent

24 Perspective

An Outlook on Outlook

But do not forget this one thing, dear friends: With the Lord a day is like a thousand years, a thousand years are like a day (2 Peter 3:8).

Dear Graduate,

Have you heard the ancient Hindu story about the six blind men who were brought to "see" an elephant?

"It's very like a wall," said the first man as he touched the side of the elephant.

"No, it's more like a spear," said the second man as he stroked the elephant's tusk.

But when the third man felt the elephant's trunk squirming in his hand, he said, "You are both wrong. It is more like a snake."

"Nonsense!" the fourth man shouted. Stretching his arms about one of the legs, he concluded, "This powerful beast is very like a tree!"

The fifth man, rubbing the elephant's ear, disagreed, "Even the blind can tell this animal is like a fan."

But the sixth, grabbing the tail, assured his friends that "the elephant is similar to a rope."

If these guys were right, an elephant would be a miniature museum all by itself. And yet, each man *was* right. At least from his perspective.

Point of view. How do you see things? What comes into play to affect your understanding of a person, event, or circumstance? What pet peeves irritate you and prevent you from seeing the broader picture? To what degree does another person's viewpoint affect you? How open-minded are you to changing your thinking about a particular view?

In our lead verse we can see that Peter was trying to prevent his readers from having a limited outlook. He was snapping a macro-zoom lens onto the minds of his pupils to present them with a bigger picture. He wanted to teach them how the temporal relates to the eternal. With one bombastic statement, Peter showed just how unclear our focus can be. How narrow. How prejudiced. How blind.

From our particular vantage point, we see the other guy for what he is. But, under similar conditions, we see ourselves quite differently. For instance, you have probably noticed:

When the other fellow acts abruptly, he is rude; when you do, it's nerves.

When others are set in their ways, they're stubborn, when you are, it is firmness of conviction.

When your neighbor dislikes your friend, he's prejudiced; when you don't like *his*, you're a good judge of human nature.

When he tries to treat someone especially nice, he's a showboat; when you try it, you are being thoughtful.

When he takes his time to do things well, he's a slowpoke or lazy; when you do, you are deliberate and careful.

When he spends a lot, he is a spendthrift; when you do, you're generous.

When others pick flaws in something, they're negative and critical; when you do, you're creative and constructive.

When another is mild-mannered, you call him weak; when you are, it is gentleness.

When someone else dresses especially sharp, that person is extravagant; when you do, it is good taste.

When he speaks his mind, he's spiteful; when you do, you are being frank.

When he takes great risks, he is being foolhardy; when you do, it is the "chance of a lifetime."

It's all in the circular game of perspective. Outlook dictates response. Response dictates behavior. Behavior leads to action. Action reveals character. And character determines outlook, so we're back where we started. How we see things—how we reach our conclusions—shows what kind of character we have. It also uncovers our maturity. Maybe that is why the Japanese proverb says: "Hearing a hundred times is not as good as seeing once."

In several of the other letters I've written to you, it's three points and out, but in this one I'm going to make one point and then get out. This is it:

Learn the difference between gnats and camels. When Jesus cut loose on the Pharisees one afternoon and read them the spiritual riot act, they were a blushing crew of fools. He dressed them down for their arrogance and spiritual pride. If ever men looked like monkeys in a zoo, the Pharisees did on that day. But it wasn't the Lord's goal to humiliate them. He was trying to set their perspective straight. In Matthew 23:24 he gave that classic line: "You blind guides! You strain out a gnat but swallow a camel." They could see the partial, but not the whole; they could see the insignificant, but not the necessary; they could see the trees, but not the forest. They had an outlook problem.

We should learn from the words of Jesus and Peter to have wide-open eyes and receptive minds. We should look for the bigger picture. And we should hear the other guy's point of view. Even if it means listening to some nut trying to convince us that an elephant is very like a rope.

Have the Father's eyes,
Brent

114

Three from Dear John

1, 2, and 3 John

Under special stress of emotion, the writer's paternal love, sympathy, and solicitude break out in the affectionate appellation, "little children," or yet more endearingly, "my little children". . . . He writes as light shines. Love makes the task a necessity, but also a delight.

The International Standard
Bible Encyclopedia

25 Fellowship

A Brotherhood of Strangers

We proclaim to you what we have seen and heard, so that you also may have fellowship with us. And our fellowship is with the Father and with his Son, Jesus Christ (1 John 1:3).

Dear Graduate,

Some years ago an English doctor built an experimental room to study isolation. His quiet place was 9' x 9' x 7½' and allowed a person to be totally withdrawn from the world. The soundproof cubicle was suspended by nylon rope at the top of a large building. Each volunteer was equipped with padded fur gloves and heavy woolen socks to reduce the sensation of touch. Each wore translucent goggles over his eyes to eliminate patterned vision. The doctor observed his isolated guinea pigs through a one-way screen, but they could not see out. Even their meals were eaten in the lonely box.

One by one they took their turn in the box. And the results were the same in each case. After an hour, two at the most, concentration was lost. Then came anxiety or feelings of panic. Many could not stand the aloneness for more than five hours.

To be sure, we all need our personal quiet times alone. None of us likes constant activity every minute of the day. And it's important that we pull aside to "be still" with God and ourselves. In fact, it's essential, so *some* "isolation" is necessary. But that's a far cry from what the good doctor was trying to prove.

Now for another point worth pondering: to survive in the faith, Christians must have the company of other Christians. Without fellowship there is no accountability, no challenge, no common bond, and no encouragement. John was the perfect guy to write on this topic. He was the one who leaned close to Jesus. At the foot of the cross, it was John who received the special appointment to be a replacement son for Jesus to Mary. John was the silent sidekick of Peter in the first gospel roadshow partnership. But I wonder how successful Peter would have been without the moral support of Big John.

Christian brotherhood is a major theme in this first of the John letters. Just flip through and gander at a few of the verses. The "tie that binds" was obviously on his mind. It makes a great study. Check out the whole thing sometime. Meanwhile, here are the basic nails the apostle was trying to drive home:

Fellowship is a spiritual matter. "But if we walk in the light, as he is in the light, we have fellowship with one another, and the blood of Jesus, his Son, purifies us from all sin" (1 John 1:7). Before we can enjoy better-than-superficial friendships with other believers, we must scale the jagged edges of intimacy with God. We must get to know *him.* Then we will be ready to know each other. Sin hinders our fellowship with God. And, if our fellowship with God is hindered, then our fellowship with each other is hindered, too. Therefore, sharing fellowship together is a spiritual relationship. It's more than mere friendship. You can develop a friendship with almost any-body—even creepy people. But you "fellowship" only with other Christians.

Fellowship is a caring matter. "If anyone has material posses-sions and sees his brother in need but has no pity on him, how can the love of God be in him?" (1 John 3:17). Listen, this business of fellowship is more than sitting around a table on a Friday night,

118

playing board games with a few church friends. It's more than a Sunday-afternoon game of touch football with church buddies. It's talking. Sharing. Praying. It's carrying each other, *really* carrying each other. That means when one brother is out of a job, the others pitch in to keep grub on his table and creditors away from his door. Or when one of the sisters is confined to a hospital bed, the others fix a strategy to keep her house clean and her family fed. If all you want is a pal to chat with occasionally, you're not after fellowship. Then you're looking for a little boost, but fellowship is a permanent bond.

Fellowship is a family matter. To share in this supreme circle of encouragement, a person needs to be in the family of God. This comes by faith in Jesus. Not every person who claims to have connections with God is truthful. That is why John wrote these words just on the heels of strong talk about fellowship: "Dear friends, do not believe every spirit, but test the spirits to see whether they are from God, because many false prophets have gone out into the world" (1 John 4:1). Some people think that all so-called religions should just band together because, after all, "they all believe in God." Well, we're not all spokes on the same wheel unless we have a common center. Jesus is the only way for a Christian. And he is the cornerstone of fellowship's foundation. If he is not worshiped as the only true God, then the bond of fellowship cannot be tied. That's the straight and narrow truth.

Be careful, though, not to shut out genuine disciples. Others don't have to walk our walk and talk our talk to belong to Jesus. We are terribly prone to the we're-the-only-ones-who-are-right disease. The Lord gags on that. Why? Because it leads to isolationism. And you know what that leads to—wearing furry gloves, wooly socks, and strange sunglasses, even to church.

Simply your brother,
Brent

26 Pursuit

Running in His Shoes

Anyone who runs ahead and does not continue in the teaching of Christ does not have God; whoever continues in the teaching has both the Father and the Son (2 John 9).

Dear Graduate,

If any of these letters were more important than the others, I suppose it would be this one. The one thing I would tell you if I could tell you nothing else is "Follow hard after God." Pursue him. Seek him and he will be found. Do not keep him at arm's length. God should not be boxed up like an incidental treasure and stuffed behind other prettier objects. Lesser priorities should never be crowded into his room until there isn't space enough for him to sit on the throne. God is generous, indeed. He gives and gives. But there is one thing he will not share: his Lordship.

It is wonderful to know God, but to pursue him is an adrenaline drench. It requires a passionate thirst to become intimate friends with the King of kings. We must simultaneously endure the agony of letting him stoop to our lowly plane while we mountaineer to his heights of glory. And this hot pursuit must be like the psalmist's, who said: "As the deer pants for streams of water, so my soul pants for you, O God. My soul thirsts for God, for the living God. When can I go and meet with God?" (Ps. 42:1–2). In olden days this was the supreme goal of men and women. Listen to the way A. W. Tozer described their electricity in his classic, *The Pursuit of God:*

> Come near to the holy men and women of the past and you will soon feel the heat of their desire after God. They mourned for Him, they prayed and wrestled and sought for Him day and night, in season and out, and when they had found him the finding was all the sweeter for the long seeking. Moses used the fact that he knew God as an argument for knowing Him better. "Now, therefore, I pray thee, if I have found grace in thy sight, show me now thy way, that I may know thee, that I may find grace in thy sight"; and from there he rose to make the daring request, "I beseech thee, show me thy glory." God was frankly pleased by this display of ardor, and the next day called Moses into the mount, and there in solemn procession made all His glory pass before him.

Whew! How magnificent! And just think, Moses had no Bible. He didn't have a church. His place of worship was extraordinary, but quite primitive. Moses had no study helps; he certainly didn't receive a spiritual book of letters for graduation. This great deliverer had never been to a seminar on spiritual growth, and if he had the benefit of a discipleship partner, we have no record of it. Still, he came to know God to a degree so far beyond what we have imagined that it boggles our brains to compare ourselves—even though he was only a human being as are we all.

What made the difference? Moses pursued God. Fearlessly. Faithfully. First and foremost. He prayed. He fasted. He longed for God like a child longs for his first bicycle. We sense that Moses would have died if he could not have drawn near to God. In the end, the meekest man who ever lived—outside of Jesus—died high on Nebo Hill, still thirsting for Jehovah. That is the difference.

Satan is clever. Give him credit. The ruler of hell has kept his elves working overtime to devise a million things to distract us. Between television and movies alone, we have enough to occupy all our time until Jesus comes. Not to mention music concerts, baseball and football games, romance novels, and computer games.

Easy! Easy! I'm not condemning those things. I'm simply saying that they have the potential to absorb too much of our time if they aren't kept in a proper perspective. Valuable time that could be spent in pursuit of God.

Let me close with this brief story about a very insecure military man. One day he was promoted from major to colonel and was ushered into his new office. He was proud of his achievement as he sat in the new surroundings. Suddenly there came a knock at the door. He said, "Come in." A corporal walked in and saluted. Appearing very businesslike, the colonel said, "Just a minute, I have to finish this phone call." He picked up the receiver, pushed line one, and began talking, "I'm sorry about the interruption, General. Now, where were we? Oh, yes, sir, I will take care of it. Well, yes, we are good friends. Yes, I will call the president. No problem, I'll do it immediately after I finish talking to you, General. You're welcome, sir." The colonel set the receiver down, turned his attention to the corporal, and asked, "What can I do for you?" He answered, "Well, sir, I just came in to connect your telephone."

Like the colonel, there are many Christians who put on the appearance that they really have a hotline to heaven. By their behavior we are given to believe they are best buddies with Jesus, but privately they barely know him. If you were to mention "pursuit" to them, they would think of last night's cops-and-robbers show, which ended with a dynamic car chase. To put it bluntly, they need their "sky phone" connected. The Moses way.

Stay thirsty,
Brent

 **Imitation**

The Real McCoy

Dear friend, do not imitate what is evil but what is good.
Anyone who does what is good is from God. Anyone who
does what is evil has not seen God (3 John 11).

Dear Graduate,

It has been said that imitation is the sincerest form of flattery. The fashion industry thrives on that idea. People subconsciously want to be alike. Or at least they don't want to be too different from people they think are "important." If you are popular with your crowd, you can wear acid-washed jeans and pretty soon everybody's doing it. Or rip the pocket off. Give it a few months and clothiers will manufacture them that way to keep up with the demand. Certain people could wear their shoes untied and it would catch on. They could use no shoestrings and weeks later would have a following.

People are so much like sheep. I don't know where the term "copy cat" comes from, but maybe we should change it to "copy sheep." They are the ultimate imitators. Several years ago when I was pastoring in a small rural community in Kansas, land of Dorothy and Toto, I noticed a flock of sheep in a pasture along my travel route. One afternoon I stopped and watched them frolic in the field. The longer I watched, the more I understood why the Lord refers to us as sheep.

One of the bigger fellows seemed to control the whole group. One minute he would eat grass, then they would all eat grass. The next minute he would run over next to the fence, and the rest would follow suit. Moments later, the ringleader hustled to the pond for a drink. The "copy sheep" were fast on his heels, clomping like a herd of buffalo to see who would be first to follow. Finally, the boss ram tore suddenly across the field and accidentally fell into a shallow ditch. His clones were running so closely behind him that they fell in, too. Then came the funniest part. The ones who weren't foolish enough (or fast enough) to fall in with the leader, carefully climbed down into the ditch to join everybody else. That was one of the stupidest sights I've ever seen—a whole flock of sheep standing in and around a gully into which their fearless leader had fallen, awaiting his next brilliant move. If I hadn't seen it myself, I probably wouldn't have believed it.

Jesus is the Chief Shepherd. We are called to imitate *him,* not the rest of the flock. The world is supposed to have a clear picture of Jesus by just observing us. It's up to us to make them say, "Is it live or is it Memorex?"

Not only do John's letters hit hard with this theme, but our other good friend, the apostle Paul, had some words to the same effect: "You became imitators of us and of the Lord . . ." (1 Thess. 1:6). He tied this thought together in two other letters. He told the church in Corinth to "imitate me" (1 Cor. 4:16), and instructed the Ephesians, "Be imitators of God . . ." (Eph. 5:1). Paul was teaching the early Christians to copy his behavior as long as *he* was copying Jesus.

I am reminded of John Robinson's famous charge to the Pilgrims as they were about to board the *Mayflower* for America in 1620:

I charge you before God that you follow me no further than you have seen me follow the Lord Jesus Christ. If God reveals anything to you by any other instrument of His, be as ready to receive it as you were to receive any truth by my ministry, for I am verily persuaded that the Lord hath more truth yet to break out of His Holy Word.

As we seek to imitate the Lord Jesus Christ, two things must stick in our minds:

We are not perfect. Easy to remember. Right? Not for some people. They copy just enough to make them act like pious super-saints. Actually it is quite hard to ditto Jesus. It isn't like doing a good John Wayne or Ronald Reagan impression. Are we talking dynamite stuff, like walking on water and turning a few loaves into the Manor Bakery? No, not really. Jesus doesn't want us to emulate his miracles; he wants us to emulate his personhood. His behavior. His character. Still, we will fail, for to err is human—and to totally flub up is even more natural.

The Holy Spirit does it. If we ever do snap off a good imitation of Jesus, it is only because the Holy Spirit was there giving us the power and ability. No one—I mean *no one!*—has the smoothness to copy Jesus without the help of the Spirit. He is the Source; we are the vessel. He flows through us and makes us a channel of blessing. If we try to copy Jesus apart from God's Spirit, do you know what happens? You got it. Ditchville! With the rest of the sheep.

Show Jesus to the world,
Brent

Postcards of Love

Philemon; Jude

[*Philemon:*] *The charm and beauty of this epistle have been universally recognized. . . . One of the chief elements of value in it is the picture it gives us of a Christian home in the apostolic days; the father and mother well known for their hospitality, the son a man of position and importance in the church, the coming and going of the Christian brethren, and the life of the brotherhood centering about this household.*

Charles Smith Lewis

[*Jude:*] *On every hand today the great apostacy so frequently mentioned in the New Testament is making its advance. Every believer needs to know what God has to say about this subject. Hence, as a textbook the book of Jude is unsurpassed.*

John Phillips

# 28 Usefulness

The Courage to Try

Formerly he was useless to you, but now he has become useful both to you and me (Philemon 11).

Dear Graduate,

Napoleon firmly believed repetition to be the only serious principle of rhetoric. He knew what the best of teachers have long employed: ideas and truths must be restated over and again. Just because one person understands a point doesn't mean everyone instantly grasps it.

Repetition is essential to good learning, because it takes time to absorb new facts and comprehend new ideas. It even takes time for old ideas to finally sink in. Mind you, the repetition should be more than a dull cadence of the same words. To be effective, repetition requires the skillful turning of fresh phrases.

Throughout his almost-postcard-in-length letter to Philemon, Paul repeated from a baker's dozen of angles how Onesimus the slave had become useful. He emphasized it over and over. Paul wanted to make sure Philemon didn't take some drastic measure with his runaway slave. (Sorry, we don't have time to get into a full-blown discussion about the evils of slavery. I know it is confusing to read about slavery in the Bible, but it was simply an aspect of their culture.) Anyway, Paul was repetitious about Onesimus's "usefulness."

Now it's my turn to be repetitious. The principle I'm going to put across here isn't a new one. You may have heard it stated before in any one of a thousand ways. This is it: "You can be as useful as you want to be." That means even if you have handicaps (or think you have). As Henry Ford said: "Think you can, think you can't—either way you're right!" But usefulness requires more than thinking.

You may be saying to yourself, "Yeah, it takes talent, skill, and pizzazz to go far in this world." Wrong. Dead wrong. Not that talent, skill, and pizzazz will hurt your chances, but they aren't essential if you long to be "useful." Notice I did not say "successful." The most valuable—and useful—people have attained certain indispensable qualities. Successful people are not always useful; but useful people are the only true successes. So if you long to be useful, master three little ingredients:

Yieldedness. How submitted are you to the Holy Spirit? That's the $64,000 question. Because here's some bold print: God doesn't need smart, talented, outstanding, famous, or powerful people. He needs humble people, and those are the ones he uses most often. He gets a kick out of astonishing the worldly wise by exalting the humble. It's not a matter of what you have the ability to do; it's a matter of what you're willing to let God do through you.

A committee of ministers was once discussing the possibility of having D. L. Moody, the great revivalist, hold a city-wide crusade. Finally, one young minister who opposed having Mr. Moody stood up and said: "Why Moody? Does he have a monopoly of the Holy Spirit?" Dead silence filled the room. Then a godly old minister spoke up: "No, but the Holy Spirit has a monopoly of him." Yieldedness to God's will is the first and key ingredient of usefulness.

Availability. You can't be used if you aren't there. Put yourself at God's disposal and he will find a place for you. Some folks remain unused because they are busy elsewhere. Like my favorite poet, Mr. Anonymous, writes:

130

I'll go where you want me to go, dear Lord,
Real service is what I desire;
I'll say what you want me to say, dear Lord,
But don't ask me to sing in the choir.

I'll say what you want me to say, dear Lord,
I like to see things come to pass;
But don't ask me to teach boys and girls, dear Lord,
I'd rather just stay in my class.

I'll do what you want me to do, dear Lord,
I yearn for your kingdom to thrive;
I'll give you my nickels and dimes, dear Lord,
But please don't ask me to tithe.

I'll go where you want me to go, dear Lord,
I'll say what you want me to say;
I'm busy just now with myself, dear Lord,
I'll help you some other day.

Effort. Laziness is next to worthlessness. Before you can do, you first must try. If you will not muster the courage to try, you have already failed. Useful people are not nearly as bright as they are dutiful. "Work! Work! Work! Go! Go! Go! Try! Try! Try!" is their motto. Doers, movers, and shakers can't help but be useful.

Some people just keep trying. Over and over. They repeat their hard work. Again and again. They give it their best shot. Time after time. They are so repetitious they would have made Napoleon tired. But they sure are useful!

Make yourself useful,
Brent

 **Zeal**

The "Now" Breed

Dear friends, although I was very eager to write to you about the salvation we share, I felt I had to write and urge you to contend for the faith that was once for all entrusted to the saints (Jude 3).

Dear Graduate,

One of the reasons I like writing to you is this: you have zeal. Sure, sometimes you act without knowledge or forethought. But I think you have a fire to change the world. To do something great and lasting, and make a difference. I would much rather associate with someone like that than a never-fanatical robot who lost his ardor twenty years ago. You're a part of the "now" breed.

A zealot is a monomaniac—crazy about one thing, one cause, one goal, or one person. He tends to filter all of life through his highest priority. He is biased toward that one thing he considers most worth living for. We're not talking mild enthusiasm here. No, a monomaniac is a *raging* enthusiast. He is fervent and active and ardent.

Get a load of Jude. There was a monomaniac if I ever saw one. The guy was totally wrapped up in spreading God's message. Notice the key words in our lead verse: "very eager," "I felt I had to write," "urge you," "contend." Whoa! Now that is serious zeal! If Jude didn't burn with a white-hot fire for God, nobody did.

That's a real need of our present day. American churches need fired-up disciples. We've seen enough of the dead and dry ones in action to sufficiently run down a self-winding watch. We need *you*. Young blood. Old blood is okay, too, as long as it's not tired blood. And we must guard against zeal that runs out of control. Otherwise, foolishness will smother even the best of causes. Like when James and John suggested fire from heaven as a remedy for the Samaritan town that didn't welcome Jesus on his trip to Jerusalem (Luke 9:51–56). They received a funny nickname to remind them of their unbridled zeal: Sons of Thunder.

Let's get a few things straight about monomania:

There is a wrong kind. Paul was zealous even before he became a believer—he persecuted the church (Phil. 3:6). Zeal is wrong when the priority is wrong, and it is wrong when the motivation is wrong. A right thing done for a poor reason—no matter how much enthusiasm spills out—is displeasing to God. The end never justifies the means, according to God. But godly zeal gets all its ducks in a row. A proper cause propelled by a pure motive and bubbling enthusiasm is the winning combination.

You will be misunderstood. Jesus was a zealot. And what did it get him? People said he was "demon-possessed" (John 7:20). They said he was nuts (Mark 3:21). Jesus boiled (the Greek verb for *zeal* means "to boil") with holy heat for righteousness. Remember when he went into the temple where the money-changers were running their version of the Jerusalem Stock Exchange? John 2:17 says that Jesus was consumed with zeal on that day. But, as perfectly balanced as Jesus was, many people considered him a kook. Jesus told his disciples that the servant is not different from the master (Matt. 10:24). Guess what that means. Right! If you're zealous for God, there will be those who call you a religious nut. Expect it.

Zeal must be protected. If not fanned and fueled, the flames of fervor can flicker down to a few feeble embers. There's nothing duller than a tepid Christian. He does not impress even his own generation. Only John-the-Baptist types do. It was said of him: "John was a lamp that burned and gave light, and you chose for a time to enjoy his light" (John 5:35). Like the brilliant missionary Henry Martyn said when he first stood on Indian soil: "Now let me burn out for God." There are a lot of "burnouts" around today, but not many of them are burning out for God. Discouragement has snuffed out their fire. When zeal is flagging, pour on some fresh fuel—the oil of God's Spirit. Then jump into the ocean of *his* fire!

I've got some friends waiting to meet me at the golf course (something I'm trying to be less zealous about), so let me close with T. C. Hamlet's poem about two frogs, one that was zealous and one that was not.

> Two frogs fell into a can of cream,
> Or so I've heard it told;
> The sides of the can were shiny and steep,
> The cream was deep and cold.
>
> "O, what's the use?" croaked No. 1.
> "Tis fate; no help's around.
> Goodbye, my friends! Goodbye, sad world!"
> And weeping still, he drowned.
>
> But No. 2 of sterner stuff,
> Dog-paddled in surprise,
> The while he wiped his creamy face
> And dried his creamy eyes.
>
> "I'll swim awhile, at least," he said—
> Or so I've heard he said;
> "It really wouldn't help the world
> If one more frog were dead."
>
> An hour or two he kicked and swam,
> Not once he stopped to mutter,
> But kicked and kicked and swam and kicked
> Then hopped out, via butter!

Make holy butter,
Brent

 # 30 Amen

Let It Be!

> . . . to the only God our Savior be glory, majesty, power and authority, through Jesus Christ our Lord, before all ages, now and forevermore! Amen! (Jude 25).

Dear Graduate,

Do the people in your church make noise? I don't mean shuffling feet or rustling books and papers. Do they shout out agreements with the pastor while he's preaching? Have you ever heard a loud, hearty "Amen!" from a baritone-voiced man during—actually during!—the worship service? This practice is unheard of in some assemblies and thought to be a rather crude instrument of approval. In other groups a mere "Amen" would be considered mild, compared to all the other whooping going on.

As for myself, I like clapping. It's lively and noisy and it seems to better fit the bill for our culture. I've heard too many interruptive "Amens" said at the wrong time to be very tickled about the prospect of more. During one such sermon, I was making the delicate but true point that people who reject Christ will spend an eternity in everlasting torment apart from God. An eager listener shouted, "Amen, brother!" Well, that wasn't a good time for amening.

The word *amen* means "so be it" or "let it be." Bless his little heart, my zealous supporter probably meant "Yes, that's true," but his untimely outburst made it sound more like "Yeah, let 'em burn." If amening even slightly parallels applause, can you imagine people clapping gleefully when the preacher says that the ungodly are going to hell? Not too slick, but that has happened to me more times than I can count. So you can see why I'm an applause man myself, rather than an Amen-er.

"All right, Earles, what does this have to do with me?" you may want to ask. Good question. Let me ask you one in return: "How do you determine what words and actions will receive your 'Amen'"? I don't mean during church services, but in everyday life. Not that you actually say it aloud, but that you approve. You see, what "Amen" boils down to is convictions, and that has a lot to do with you.

We crave people with convictions. Tough codgers who won't back down from a firmly held principle. Mind you, even spiritual convictions may vary from one person to the next. And if my convictions aren't identical to yours, that doesn't necessarily make one of us less worthy. But if either of us compromises something we believe in deeply, it is a sin. Romans 14:23 affirms that whatever does not come from faith is sin.

Therefore, if you are going to live an "amen kind of life," you need personal convictions. "And how does one go about developing those personal convictions?" you probably wonder. Glad you asked. I'll explain:

What does God's Word say? Read the owner's manual and follow the instructions. If the Bible says, "No premarital sex," say "Amen!" by living in obedience. When it confirms the sanctity of human life, say "Amen!" by being pro-life instead of pro-choice. Of course, in some matters the Bible is not completely specific, such as: attending movies, where to draw the line with your music tastes, being fashionable without being worldly, and the role of Christians in politics. Study such "gray areas" for yourself and be "fully convinced in [your] own mind" (Rom. 14:5).

Can you hear the Spirit? I don't mean with an audible voice. Can you sense his promptings? Like the still, small voice Elijah heard. One of the Holy Spirit's jobs is to convict (John 16:8–11). That convicting produces convictions. The Spirit jabs us in the conscience and says, "Don't accept that. Speak up for God! Stand strong for truth and righteousness." Sensitive Christians can feel his presence. Not a mushy, gushy feeling that causes you to lose control of yourself. But a steady, supportive presence that inspires the courage to do right.

How about others' convictions? Here's a good one. Should you pattern your convictions after someone else's? I wouldn't advise it. You may want to listen, learn, and adopt a few, but make sure your convictions are your very own. Don't fall into the trap of having to run to another person to explain what *you* believe. That is fine for new disciples, but not mature ones.

Do convictions change? Unless you plan to stay the same for the rest of your life (a boring thought), some of your convictions are bound to change. You may find ten years from now that you will fight to the death for something you presently consider unimportant. If not to the death, at least to a severe bruising. And it is likely you will discard a few beliefs you currently wave as a banner. But Jesus never changes, truth never changes, some beliefs never change, and faith never changes. These are absolutes. Another one is that personal convictions change through the years.

Why you may even shout "Amen!" in a church service someday.

Live the Word,
Brent

137

31 Footnotes

Famous Last Words

My love to all of you in Christ Jesus. Amen (1 Cor. 16:24).

Dear Graduate,

Paul always ended his letters with kind remembrances and thoughtful niceties. I want my last letter to you to be unusual. Since it sort of stands on its own apart from the other sections, I'll let it be a summary. But not a bland, boring summary like some books have. No, this ending calls for something spicy. The kind of thing that you will want to come back to for reference whenever you're reading these letters a second or third time. The kind of thing that adds juicy flavor. Like quotes.

"What?" you're probably frowning. Yes, quotes. Delicious quotes. I love them. The carefully spun sentences of articulate people really get my gray matter moving. So let me share ten of my favorite quotes with you. Not just random citations, but ten specific sayings to help us review the main sections we've covered. Here are the quotable quotes:

I hate quotations. Tell me what you know (Ralph Waldo Emerson). What a perfect way to start! That's the mind-set Paul had when he wrote the Romans his great Declaration of Dependence. No beating around the bush. He was simply saying, "This is sin. We are sinners. Jesus is the remedy. Trust him. Live victoriously. God will take care of you." He spared them the quotes and told them what he knew. And now it's all there for us.

Always do right. This will gratify some people, and astonish the rest (Mark Twain). Paul said this to the Corinthians. He said it in a hundred ways, but this is what he meant. How perfectly fitting for us as we listen to Paul, that special pen pal, woo us and warn us to get on the straight road and stay there.

No matter what a man's past may have been, his future is spotless (John R. Rice). Thank God. There is grace for those who cry for an escape from corruption; there is peace for those who choose to be single-minded. The apostle wrote to tell us this in his early church newsletters.

Some men see things as they are and say, "Why?"; I dream things that never were and say "Why not?" (Robert Kennedy). How often has my soul been stirred to dream wondrous dreams by this thought—and to expect them to come true! The Thessalonians needed such a motivation. Paul taught them to scrutinize and find it. Then he carried them on the wings of Jesus' coming to compel them. Us, too!

When I was a young man I observed that nine out of ten things I did were failures. I didn't want to be a failure, so I did ten times more work (George Bernard Shaw). That's how Paul instructed young Timothy and Titus in the Pastoral Epistles. And it is the same lesson we must follow if we would become top guns.

Amusement is the happiness of those that cannot think (Alexander Pope). But Hebrews is the thinking-Christian's letter. It is for the tough and mature. It is about legacy and heritage. It is for those who are "amused" by challenge.

Young people tell what they are doing, old people tell what they have done, and fools what they wish to do (French proverb). If I didn't know better, I would guess James wrote this. His candid letter is so much like one long proverb that it at once lures its readers and knifes through their consciences with "Do something! Hurry, do it now!"

Depend upon it, friends, if a straight line will not pay, a crooked one will not ("John Ploughman," pseudonym of C. H. Spurgeon). An excellent way to sum up Peter's words about exploiters, and to sharpen our perspective.

God had only one Son, and He was a poor missionary and a physician. A poor, poor imitation of Him I am, or wish to be (David Livingstone). Doesn't that sound almost like John? So tender. So thoughtful. So humble. Like he teaches us to be in his three letters.

Anybody who thinks the sky is still the limit has no imagination (Anonymous, in *Saturday Evening Post*). This is for all zealots who would live "amen lives" of usefulness, as recorded in the postcards of Philemon and Jude.

There you have my summary. My footnotes, if you will. Thank you for letting me be more personal than a usual-type book. Now go out and carve into history some "famous last words" of your own. Step into a waiting world—and live an unforgettable life!

> Lord, fill my mouth with
> worthwhile stuff and nudge
> me when I've said enough,
> Brent

P.S. You now owe me thirty-one letters!